All This…
and Heaven too

Kathleen A. Jackson

DEDICATION

I lovingly dedicate this book to my boyfriend of the past fifty years. Falling in love with you has made my life "All this and Heaven too."

Thank you for your loving leadership. You gave our children godly borders that kept them safe until they could grow up and love God-not because they *had to*, but because they wanted to love Him! A parent has no greater joy than to know her children walk in truth (3 John 1:4). They saw in your life the best way to live their life.

Thank you for making dailiness so special with your thoughtfulness.

Thank you for teaching me how to forgive; that principle has kept me blessed rather than bitter.

Thank you for teaching me to be a soul winner. The obedience to that command keeps my faith fresh and brings purpose into every day.

Thank you that we know each other so well that we speak each other's thoughts. Every time I hold your hand, my heart whispers, "All this and Heaven too!"

CONTENTS

1 THANKS, CLINT, YOU SAVED MY LIFE

My thirsty soul's greatest need is Living Water. In Psalm 42:2, David penned, "My soul thirsteth for God."

Jesus invites me to the Spring of Living Water. Like the woman at the well, I drink in salvation and know the cleansing rinse of forgiveness. I know the washing away of my sins; my soul drinks and is refreshed. And while my soul is saved for eternity, like my body's need for physical water, the refreshment of my soul and spirit is a daily need. So our Savior calls us to "worship" in spirit and in truth. Worshipping is to the dry, thirsty soul what water is to the dry, thirsty body. So why do we Christians exist with a "withered on the Vine" soul, when worshipping in spirit and in truth is available to us?

1. We forget!
A couple years ago we were vacationing with Tina, Aaron, and the grandsons. Tina and I took Jack and Wil (ages 4 and 3 yrs.) and Clint to the pool. Carefully we

secured the lifejackets on the young boys, and they splashed into the pool. At one point Jackson needed to use the restroom, so quickly Tina helped him take off his lifejacket, and ushered him toward the restroom. A few minutes later, Clint was standing on the edge of the pool's deep end with his toes curled around the edge of the cement. He was getting ready to show off his patented "Clint belly-flopper." He waited to make sure everybody was watching, counted down 3-2-1, and slammed <SPLASH> into the water. Jackson had just come around the corner and saw Clint's cool "dive." He hollered, "WOW! I can do that too!" and with three big bounds he leaped and catapulted himself into the deep end. Of course, he had forgotten that he had not put on his life vest! Tina and I had been lounging with our ice coffees and simultaneously shout, "NOOOO!" Like a bad dream caught in quicksand, this Grandma body couldn't get up. Tina was yelling "Clint, grab Jack's arm!" He had already gone under twice, was gulping and gagging water, and his eyes were as big as saucers! Clint with two strokes reached him and literally yanked him up. Tina who had leaped in the pool (while Grandma was still struggling to get out of the lounge chair) reached him, and together with Clint, she rescued one frightened, little boy. Huddled in a beach blanket, tears coming down his cheeks, Jackson said to Clint, "Thanks Clint, You saved my life!" Afterward, Tina instructed Jack, "You can't forget like that, it could have been much worse!"

Girls, in our sin-born nature, we follow what everybody else is doing. "I can do that too," we shout like Jack. It takes us into a flying leap into the polluted pool of life, and we are in way over our head! But a loving Savior leaps in after us (actually, He is there before us, because He knows us). He is there to lift us up and set our feet on the Solid Rock. Psalm 62:2, He saves our soul from eternal damnation in a lake of fire, and He saves this life of mine from being ruined and wasted. My aching soul shouts, "Thank you Jesus, You saved my life!"

For the rest of the vacation we heard Jackson telling anyone who would listen, "My Uncle Clint saved my life!" When you truly experience salvation you just have to tell others – there is nothing worse than being in over your head, and there is nothing better than being rescued!

If you are a saved soul but not a daily washed soul, there is something you have forgotten. Ask the Holy Spirit of God to point it out. Psalm 139:23-24 "Search me, O God, and know my heart: try me, and know my thoughts: And see if there be any wicked way in me, and lead me in the way everlasting."

.

2 INFLUENCED

Once as Jackson and Wil were staying overnight I was helping in the tooth brushing regiment as we prepared for bedtime. With a mouthful of toothpaste, Jackson spit out, "Grandma, if you want to be a green monster you have to turn the water off!" "What?!" It was repeated with more toothpaste spatters. "Green," was the operative word and I knew he was echoing a, "save the earth," mantra. Later I found out it was from a PBS cartoon. So I laughed and said, "You are right, Jackson, I'm always after Clint to turn off the water as he brushes his teeth; but I just want you to know, I am a 'drill here, drill now' kind of Granny!" Of course, he did not know what that meant, but it made me feel good to say it, and he was just happy I turned off the water.

It really irritates me, how "influenced" our children are from television and media. As a matter of fact, Tina told me that Jack informed her that they should ride their bikes to church because it saves energy!

INFLUENCED! Wow! Dear sisters, there is something more important than wasting water, and it is drinking from the Springs of Living Water! A clean heart is more vital than clean water; knowing the One who made the very earth I put my "footprint" on, is what our children need to know. So all day we must influence, talk about, point out, rejoice, praise, and give thanks to the One who made heaven and earth. That is how others, especially our children and grandchildren, will know, it is good to live green, but it is a PRIVILEGE TO LIVE CLEAN. Our wonderful Father wants to accomplish that in our everyday life. "Create in me a clean heart O God; and renew a right spirit within me." Psalm 51:10

3 TREAT BAGS

Can you believe how quickly time goes! Talk about our life being a vapor, I think I can see it evaporating right in front of my eyes...or perhaps that is the steam from the summer day. Anyways, I am putting together a treat bag for a friend. Her surgery went well and she is recouping. The treat bag got me thinking... whether called "Aunt Kathy" or -now- "Grammy," I have always been known for my "treat bags." The idea was born out of "drama-trauma." Back when the girls were young, we enjoyed lots of cousin days with Karissa and Katie. Whenever it was time to leave, the weeping and wailing began. It was "separation-anxiety." One time as Karissa began to tear up because it was time to go, I quickly said, "Wait! Wait! Aunt Kathy has a treat, but you can only get it when it is time to go." I ran into the kitchen, slopped some canned frosting on a graham cracker, stuffed it into a baggy and drew a heart on it. It was just the thing that stopped the separation-anxiety! It had worked so successfully that even grown up my nieces still want their treat bag when they leave. The grandkids know Grandma will have a gummy worm or pretzels in a bag for when they leave. It is a reminder: "You don't need to be sad, we had a great time, and you can come back soon. Now taste these goodies as you leave and remember our good togetherness-time."

My, how our Father wishes we had more "separation-anxiety" for our time with Him! He wants me to yearn to be with Him. He has treat bag delights. Psalm 68:19a, "Blessed be the Lord, who daily loadeth us with benefits." He wants me to take His Word with me when I "leave" remembering the sweet time we had together in prayer (conversation). If this sounds foreign or strange, it is because you are not practicing it. David says in Psalm 103:2, "Bless the Lord, O my soul, and forget not all his benefits:" Psalm 103:5a, "Who satisfieth my mouth with good things…"

My Lord's treat bags to me are just for me. I put a crossword puzzle book in my friend's treat bag, because that is what she likes. My Father knows me (Psalm 139). He knows what to put in my treat bag. Psalm 100:3-4 says, "Know ye that the Lord He is God: it is He that hath made us, and not we ourselves; … Enter into His gates with thanksgiving, and into His courts with praise:" There is my instruction! It is what God wants me to take with me, from my time with Him. I can take what He has given me everywhere …thanksgiving! Whether it is to the store, or to work, or in tasks from laundry to pulling weeds. I ought not let anything "unthankful" come out of my mouth.

It is a choice. Give "thanks" and you won't believe how much better your day "tastes," because you are eating from His treat bag. Have you picked up your "treat bag" from your heavenly Father today? He has filled it just for you.

4 DEVILED EGGS

The woman at the well went to the well because she wanted "to get her fill of water." Jesus went to the well because He knew she really needed to be filled with worship. Which brings me to my question, "Do we really know what we need?" Often, we don't. Our Father gives us the Holy Spirit to reveal it, if we will just ask.

It reminds me of the deviled eggs Trina and I once made. I had never made them, because I have an egg allergy. We had no recipe, but Trina was with me, so knowing that she could "taste" them, and knowing the basic ingredients, and knowing Doug, Clint and Daniel love them….I said, "Let's do this!" We boiled 7 eggs, one extra to taste or ruin, mashed down the yokes, added ¼ cup of mayo, strained relish, salt, pepper…hmmm "Go ahead, taste it Trina." "It's bland Mom." Well, I knew how to fix that. We both love mustard, so instead of adding 1-2 tablespoons, I reasoned "Let's balance out the mayo with the mustard." I added ¼ cup of mustard, then with a flash of culinary inspiration I said, "I KNOW what will put the devil in these deviled eggs:

9

crushed red pepper! Doug and I like "spicy." I knew, we liked horse-radish, loved that smoky-under flavor, so in went a tablespoon of that; and we stirred it up. "Okay Trina, try that." With a teaspoon in hand, she tried it. The teaspoon clattered into the sink, hands flew around her own neck, eyes bugged out and began to tear, and gagging sounds choked from her mouth. Later we laughed and came to the same conclusion: I did not KNOW what the eggs needed.

When it comes for the recipes of living today, know that we do not naturally KNOW! When I live today with what comes naturally, my day, and the people in my day, are going to take on the face of Trina tasting those eggs. Now listen to what the Lord wants us to know! This is so good, I Corinthians 2:11-16, "For what man knoweth the things of a man, save the spirit of man which is in him? Even so the things of God knoweth no man, but the Spirit of God. Now we have received, not the spirit of the world, but the Spirit which is of God; that we might know the things that are freely given. Which things also we speak, not in words which man's wisdom teacheth, but which the Holy Ghost teacheth; comparing spiritual things with spiritual. But the natural man receiveth not the things of the Spirit of God: for they are foolishness unto him: neither can they know them, because they are spiritually discerned…but we have the mind of Christ."

That is great! You and I can KNOW what we really need. Like a glass of cold water on a hot day; your soul will say, "Ahhhh!" Have you found God's recipe for your day today? Open His Book. Some of my favorite recipes for tasty loving is found in the book of Ephesians. Copy them, taste them, and serve them up to others.

5 CUPBOARD

So how does cleaning out a cupboard make a gramma cry? Because it wasn't just ANY cupboard, it was the "grandchildren's" cupboard! Over seven years ago it was emptied of dishes and platters as I lovingly, carefully stocked it with toys that stacked, rolled, and squeaked. It was right in the living room, so handy to pull out a baby blanket and rattles to amuse and entertain that miracle called, "grandchild."

How fun to keep up with every stage from puzzles to magic markers to candy land. But the years flew by on sneakers that light up, and the cupboard was used less and less. This summer was filled with bats and balls and bikes; even Caleb, our youngest grandchild, wanted little to do with the cupboard.

The cupboard: as I pulled on the knobs and the hinges creaked with unuse, I "emptied" it. The slow tears mocked the speeding years. I looked at the "empty" cupboard and I whispered, "I hate empty!" Now understand, the word "hate" was never allowed in the growing up years of our children. The only exception was to say, "I hate sin." So when I say I "hate" empty, I really hate it!

The very word "empty" sounds like what it is. Look at your face when you say "empty." Why, even my lips purse and thin out, like a disapproving shrew, as I say the word. "Emp…" and then "…ty", my mouth turns down like Ebenezer.

It was just yesterday, our twin daughters, Tina and Trina, skipped down the driveway in shiny, new school shoes. They were feeling all grown up at five years old, entering the doors of our Christian school. Leaving them, Clint at three years old, climbed back into the wagon and we walked home; as we opened the front door our home whispered "empty."

So do you know what we did? We set the table for a party! We included Strawberry Shortcake, and Lemon Meringue (the girls' favorite dolls); we made their favorite food; we colored a "welcome home" banner; and had our favorite Patch cassette ready to play. We "filled" the empty with doing our jobs; we "filled" empty with meeting other people's needs as we worked through therapy time for Clint, we made treat bags for the teachers. And before we knew it, I watched four little dancing feet come down the drive way! The children were coming home! And my heart was FULL with their presence.

Are you in an "empty" spot? "Life" is so full of them: don't get stuck in it! Live with the anticipation of our Blessed Hope! Fill it with joyful service. "Whatsoever thy hand findeth to do, do it with all thy might!" Serve one another and serve your Lord with gladness. And before you know it, we children are going HOME! And guess what? Our Father is preparing a table for us. Psalm 23:5 assures us that He is fixing a feast! Revelations 19:9 tells us that He has colored a banner for me. It spells out "Love" (Song of Solomon 2:4), and oh, the New Song we will be singing!

Best of all, these lips will never be shaped with the word "empty." These ears will never hear "empty." These eyes will never shed a tear over "empty." Through all eternity our hearts will be FULL. We will be filled with the fullness of God (Ephesians 3:19) because all the children are home, and we live in His Presence.

6 SPIRITUAL CARTWHEELS

"Grandma, watch what I can do!" and with childhood nimbleness, Jackson executes a cartwheel. Wanting to spread the upside-down joy of a cartwheel, he offers, "Grandma, just put your hands in the grass, and your feet in the air and now lift your body…it's easy!" "Jackson, I'd love to but I hurt my back and I'm having a hard time just tying my shoes."

I really had hurt my back; I could kick myself, but that would hurt too. I knew how I did it…I had carried multiple pieces of furniture to the basement. They didn't feel too heavy at the time, but I should have waited for help. I was impatient as I reasoned, "I can do this," as I continued to carry more pieces. Thirty-six hours later, I HURT! I took some Motrin, and Doug kindly applied muscle relief ointment. Now I am being careful about what I pick up and carry because not only do I hurt, but I can't do what I would like to do – cartwheels excluded.

The question I want to ask you on this beautiful, "feel like a kid again" Saturday is, "when was the last time you did a cartwheel?" Not a physical one but a spiritual-cartwheel that spreads upside-down joy. Often our answer matches what I told Jackson. "I can't, I'd love to but I hurt…" The inability to 'do' can be traced back to picking up something you and I shouldn't have, and now we are feeling the effects of carrying it. Maybe it is carrying "offenses" – they seemed 'little' at the time, but they still hurt. Yes, and it will continue to weigh us down as it develops into bitterness. Jesus calls me to forgive, not just for my own healing but for the joy of living light. Matthew 11:30 teaches, 'For my yoke is easy, and my burden is light." Forget living large, I want to live light!

I thought I could handle that furniture; it didn't feel heavy at the time. I cringe when I see young moms carrying babies, car seats, diaper bags, Bibles and purses…they have no idea what carrying all that weight is doing to their body, but down the road the evidence will be clear. (All you girls over fifty are nodding your heads in agreement.)

The sin you are involved in, whether worrying or worldliness, or guilt or greed, will have immobilizing consequences in the future. Galatians 6:7 admonishes, "Be not deceived; God is not mocked: for whatsoever a man soweth, that shall he also reap." God calls us to CAST it, not carry it. I Peter 5:7 instructs, "Casting all your care upon him; for he careth for you." He also calls us to CONFESS it; do not cover it. I John 1:9 reminds us, "If we confess our sins, he is faithful and just to forgive our sins, and to cleanse us from all unrighteousness." We learn in Proverbs 28:13, "He that covereth his sins shall not prosper: but whoso confesseth and forsaketh them shall have mercy."

Thankfully, I'm doing much better today. I am taking care of the pain, applying the right ointment, and I don't hurt! I can do what I want to do.

Let me encourage you, if you got up this morning "hurting," if it's been a while since you've spiritually cart-wheeled, spreading the upside-down joy of being His child, then allow the Holy Spirit to identify the heavy weight that so easily besets you, and LAY IT ASIDE. Hebrews 12:1 encourages, "Wherefore seeing we also are compassed about with so great a cloud of witnesses, let us lay aside every weight, and the sin which doth so easily beset us, and let us run with patience the race that is set before us."

In Acts, a group of people chose to do this, and guess what? They turned the world upside down!! In Acts 17:6 we read, "...These that had turned the world upside down..." Now that is cart-wheeling! You and I can do the same; in Jackson's words (slightly paraphrased) "just put your hands in the Word, and you feet in the church and know that He will lift you up! Psalm 30:1 praises, "I will extol thee, O LORD; for thou hast lifted me up..."

I'm sure the grandkids are living their childhood Saturday. I bet they are all on their bikes – Caleb has mastered the tricycle, Jack and Wil are faster than a speeding bullet, Katelyn and Autumn fly like the wind! Well, Grandma is going to hop on her bike and fly like…maybe a strong breeze, because I have taken care of what I'm not supposed to carry (physically and spiritually). There is a world out there that needs to see a Grandma (and girls, ladies, wives, mothers, and sisters) with a child-like faith, spreading an upside-down JOY, that can only come from the inside-out. Blessed by a loving Father who heals our hurts and delights in enabling us to do what He made us to do.

7 CLUE

It is a beautiful morning outside, but I am irritated on the inside. The why of it does not matter; the what, I do know; the who, I know; the when, is this day; and the where, is inside me. It is affecting everything I do! I'm like Eeyore with the grey cloud over his head. So on this God-made blank page of a sunny day, I have already taken a grey crayon out of my box of choices and scribbled all over the page.

Last night, Autumn and I were having a "girls night." I had picked up a little, flat, bendable, girl doll with long dark hair at Cracker Barrel's 40% off corner. She had on the cutest little outfit, right down to her shoes. Guess what the first thing was that Autumn wanted to do? Strip all the layers off!! She had to see what was underneath all that stuff.

Trina had an exciting teen-girls' party last night. It was a "chocolate murder mystery!" Everyone had to come dressed as a "clue" person. Trina was Miss Peacock with a glorious blue wig and feather boas. They had a blast!

Throughout the whole evening the teams had clues to reveal "who" was the victim, and "who" was the culprit.

Here is the application: our "feelings" are clues to reveal "who" I am. They should take us to the solution, but often we stay stuck in dark rooms. Trina's whole house was lit only by candlelight. When I act or respond to my feelings they only take me to a darker place. I walk into the room of "revenge," and pick up a weapon. It is not a knife; I use something sharper, my tongue. I could go into the closet of "self-pity" and lock myself in so no one will ever hurt me again, or I could run down the hallway of "never-land," simply running away. Oh, there are so many wrong places to go, and it is so easy because all I have to do is follow my feelings.

It is easy to stay lost in the darkness. God's Words says the god of this world has blinded the minds of them which believe not, lest the light of the glorious gospel of Christ, who is the image of God, should shine unto them. The preceding verse in 2 Corinthians 4:3 states, "But if our gospel be hid, it is hid to them that are lost." Obviously the bigger picture of my "feelings" is Satan's goal to dim my Light. God's solution for my "feelings" is to direct me into His light. "Thy word is a lamp unto my feet..." (Psalm 119:105). It turns me toward His Light, and begins to reveal "what" is under all my layers, or feelings; like Autumn stripping off all the externals to see what her doll really is. The Word of God is sharp; it is a discerner of the thoughts and intents of my heart. Yikes, that is so revealing!

Yes! That is right where God means to take me, "Search me, O God and know my heart, try me and know my thoughts and see if there be any wicked way in me and lead me in the way everlasting..." (Psalm 139:23-24). Get me into the Light, O Lord; get me out of this dark room; I have a whole day to enjoy.

8 RULES

Captain Gregory was the talk of all America in 1941, because of what he invented. His invention took off like wild fire. What was it? Well, his invention was comprised of "nothing." Thin air, he invented nothing.

While you try to guess what he invented in 1941, I want to warn you about your faith, and how "rules" can turn into nothing: thin air. The purpose of rules is to allow my faith to grow. God made a rule about Sunday, honoring Him on the first day of the week. He even set up and ordained the Bible to give clear guidelines about what pleases Him.

So, we keep the rule, get everybody to church, rush, push, gripe, but they are all here! (Oh No!) In setting up rules for rearing children so they will love God, we settle into a "routine" of Christian living and scheduling. Now I am a big supporter of scheduling, especially back in my child-rearing days. Priorities have to be set, but the grave danger is working the rule to the neglect of working my faith. The truth is that what I do and say before and after church affects my children's faith even more than obeying the rule of going to church. My words and actions tell and show why I kept the rule.

Here are a couple of suggestions for living my faith, instead of living a rule. 1. Make sure your heart is clean. If your heart is too filled with "junk" your faith stays buried! 2. Sing a song or have godly music playing on the way to church. 3. Help someone "new" feel at home, be a friend. Tell the children you want to hear how they helped somebody in class or Jr. Church. 4. Pray for someone to be saved. 5. Say you're sorry if you were a "crab" getting ready for church (kids forgive so easily, but never forget hypocrisy.) 6. On the way home, share a blessing; talk about the Bible story, ask how they can put that principle in their life.

So many ways to "work" my faith over "working" a rule. When we relegate our faith to a list of rules, Jesus describes that as a form of religion, which produces nothing! Which brings us back to Gregory's invention of "nothing." Each year in the U.S. alone, the business which began on a little New England stove grosses an estimated $750 million dollars! It all started with Hanson Gregory, who noticed that his mother's fried cakes were soggy at the center. The youngster picked up a fork, and poked it through the middle of one of the cakes, and invented something which forevermore would comprise absolutely nothing, the "hole" in the doughnut!

Many of you have been saved so long, you are in the "middle" of your faith. Remember the beginning of your faith? Wow! Our glorious salvation! Our newness in Christ! So forgiven! But now, after all these decades, your faith has slipped into the easy routine of "keeping a schedule." Singing "Tell Me The Old, Old Story" has become just that, old, nothing.

Think of kids in the middle of summer. If you ask most kids "whatcha been doing?" they respond, "Oh, nothing." It wasn't like that in the beginning of summer. They had all kinds of summer plans; and the ending of summer is full of gearing up for school and sports. It's that middle time that's so dangerous. The Holy Spirit whispers, "What are you doing with your faith?" and the response is, "Oh, nothing."

James describes a "nothing" faith. Faith without works is dead, nothing. Just like our muscles, our faith needs to work. When I become discouraged or disenchanted the Holy Spirit points to those symptoms and says, "Kathy, You are working a rule; you have disengaged your faith. It's nothing! You're not going to like it!" It's like me telling you to enjoy the hole of a donut. There's nothing delightful or tasty about the hole in a donut, and neither is there anything delightful or tasty in a faith that isn't tasted. 1 Timothy 4:6 instructs that we be, "…nourished up in the words of faith…"

So I encourage you, whatever you are in the middle of today (middle places are hard) work your faith. In the middle of your marriage, SHOW your faith to your husband; in the middle of your day, love your faith; in the middle of your problem, pray you faith; in the middle of your arguing time, respond with your faith; in the middle of your happy time, sing your faith; in the middle of your praying time, pray in faith believing; in the middle of your hurting time, trust your faith.

Of course, we would never give up a donut for a hole; but dear sister, we are so easily deceived by giving up our faith for a rule! O Taste and See that the Lord is GOOD!

9 LOST AND FOUND

It was summer, and seven year old granddaughter Katelyn, raced out our doors to be with her new bff. It was a new, shiny, purple, two wheeled Schwinn! She loved her bike. They would fly like the wind. A few weeks later, a sobbing Katelyn cries, "Gramma, someone stole my bike!" Sure enough, someone had. The police were contacted, but gave very little hope that it would be found. Her daddy was out looking in the neighborhood and parks (remember, we live in Saginaw.)

So while tears were trickling down her cheeks, I took her hands and said "Katelyn, let's pray your daddy finds your bike. Even now, God knows right where it's at. But most of all, let's pray for those who stole it."

With a gasp of realization, she said, "Oh, Gramma, it would be awful to be that person. They need Jesus! Well, let's pray for that." And in that instance, her focus was taken off her loss, and redirected to someone else's need. That's a big part of the reason Jesus says pray for your enemies; and don't be overcome with evil, but overcome evil with good. That's the power of prayer. As I take God's word and implement it into my prayer life, "Father your word says, "Say not, I will do so to Him as He hath done to me" (Proverbs 24:29). It rids this deceitful and desperately wicked heart of its revenge.

Well, three hours later the door bell rang, and it was a police officer with a big smile saying to Katelyn, "I think I found something that belongs to you." Sure enough her bike was found! But Katelyn found something more valuable, more eternal, than her bike. She found the freedom from living unto the "loss." She was learning to put into practice "pray for those who despitefully use you..." which displaced the anger and injustice that wanted to find a home in her heart. Her heart could say, "Lord I trust you with this loss."

10 ALREADY HIS

"Gramma! I have something for you. Close your eyes; hold out your hands! It's just for you." Excited with the joy of giving (because the principle of giving always reaps joy) Katelyn deposited an enormous, deep purple clematis flower into my opened hands. "I picked it just for you." A dew drop was dripping and sparkling like a jewel. It was winking at me, knowing the secret that Katelyn's flower came from "my" clematis vine! She was giving to me that which was already mine. Playing into the sweet drama of the moment I exclaimed, "Oh, thank you, dear child, I will wear it in my hair!"

Later on, as I was watering my thirsty plants, I looked at my clematis that has exploded into a waterfall of cascading blossoms, and I smiled. I could see Katelyn plucking off what was already mine, to "give" to me.

Isn't that exactly what we do with our Father? He made us, sustains us (Acts 17:28), and in Him we have our being (the "way" our bodies work). All the creation is His, and as His child I pluck what is already His, and proudly present "my generosity and thoughtfulness" saying, "Father, I have something for you!" The gift I offer to Him was created by Him! The Maker of time smiles as I give Him some of my (His) time. As I pluck off the royal colored day of "Sunday" and say, "Here, Father, this is just for You."

If the tables were turned, I think I would be saying, "Really? Don't you know I MADE this day? I made it to save you from your self-absorbed life. I made it to give you rest, not just in your body (because you will run yourself ragged if left to yourself), but rest in your soul and refreshment in your spirit." Zechariah 12:1 speaks of our Creator God, "...which stretcheth forth the heavens and layeth the foundations of the earth and formeth the spirit of man within him." God made it so we could learn from His Word how to wisely live the other six days.

 Oh, the lengthy (and eye rolling) lecture I would give, if I were God. But not our Father, in parental love, He smiles as I give to Him that which is already His. Whether I give my (His) time, or my (His) resources, or my (His) abilities. "It's just for you," I stammer as I offer it to Him. He closes His eyes, holds out His hands, and receives it as a sweet smelling sacrifice! Wow!

I pick Him a bouquet from my (His) words (He that formed my mouth- Isaiah 43:7), and do you know what He does with my gift that He made! Read Malachi 3:16-17, to find out!

Remember that diamondized drop of dew on Katelyn's offered flower? Our Lord takes our (His) offered gifts and they become jewels! Could this be what I offer back to Him in that last day? When I see clearly for the first time that it was ALL His to begin with!

11 LOOK AT MY TREASURE

"Gramma! Gramma! You want to see my treasure?" "Of course, Jack." So with all the excitement of a seven year old boy, bursting with the privilege of showing something he has to someone else, he began pulling out all his weapons! "It's a treasure! Gramma, look how this works" and he pulled back the bow; "and Gramma, look at all the bullets that go into this cool nerf gun!" He put on his super hero outfit, flexed his muscles, and pronounced, "I'll save the world! And Gramma, that's not all!" Next, he pulled out a very special treasure box. It was Grandpa's old, hard-cased, locking Samsonite briefcase. Slowly, ceremoniously, he lifted the lid. Wow! It was filled with glistening marbles, and coins and dollar bills. He looked right into my eye and whispers, "Isn't that a treasure, Gramma!"

All day I smiled at the wonder of a boy and his treasure. Well, guess what, I call to you, "Girls! Girls! You wanna see my treasure?!" I am bursting with the excitement of it! We have weapons! 1 Corinthians 10:4 tells us the weapons of our warfare are mighty through God, to the pulling down of strongholds! What has a strong hold on

you today? God has a weapon that will pull it down!
Look at our super hero outfit. Isaiah 61:10 says, I will
greatly rejoice in the Lord, for my soul shall be joyful in
my God. If your soul isn't joyful, perhaps you're not
wearing what Christ has provided. He hath clothed me
with the garments of salvation, he hath covered me with
the robe of righteousness, as a bridegroom decketh
himself with ornaments and as a bride adorneth herself
with jewels. Wow! Get dressed in that today! Then open
the treasure of His Word; it is not just glistening change
(coins), it is what changes me! Isn't that a treasure!

 Lastly, there is such excitement in sharing and showing
your treasure to others. If your faith is feeling dull or
buried, start sharing it. Nothing stirs up your faith, builds
your faith, adds to your faith like sharing it. Share it with
those who need salvation, and share it with those who
are already in the family of God. Look at what happens
when you speak about your treasure; Malachi 3:16-17
says, "Then they that feared the Lord spake OFTEN
one to another; and the Lord hearkened, and heard it
and a book of remembrance was written before Him for
them that feared the Lord and that thought upon His
name. And they shall be mine, saith the Lord of hosts, in
that day when I make up my JEWELS…" Jesus looks
into my eyes and whispers, "You're my treasure!"

12 PUTTING ON LIPSTICK

"Grammmahhh?" (imagine a slightly nasally whine, and you're hearing the endearing tonal inflection of my four year old granddaughter, Autumn.) "Grammah? Whatcha doing?" "Putting on lipstick." "Whyyy?" "Because Grandpa is coming home, and I want to look pretty." "And that lipstick does that?" (Okay, stop laughing.) "Well, it helps," I respond. "Look at Grandma's lips, see how faded they are?" "Um, hum." "And see all those vertical lines that you point out when you sit on my lap and look closely at my face?" "Um Hum." "So watch as Grandma draws a new line with her lipstick; you don't see all those little lines and look how my lips change when I apply this color." "Wow Gramma, can I try those colors too?" So we applied sparkly, shiny, slicker shades from punchy pink to radiant red.

Katelyn, who at first didn't want to "do lipstick," saw how much fun we were having and joined in using all the colors too.

God has a cosmetic drawer. He has beautiful shades He wants me to apply. Psalm 90:17 tells us, "And let the beauty of the Lord be upon us…" 1 Peter tells us to be good stewards (apply what God has provided) of the manifold grace of God. The word "manifold" is also the word "multi-colored." So to "what" do we apply this multi-colored grace? Why, to the manifold temptations talked about in 1 Peter 1:6. "Whereby ye greatly rejoice though now for a season…" I have grace to apply to every wrinkled line that crosses our smoothly planned day. As I apply His grace to it, He beautifies it. As I apply God's grace to my thinking, my old mind is renewed! My old "line of reasoning" recalibrates and changes as I apply His color. My mind is "smoothed" with God's color of Truth. It's more than a topical application; it's an inside transformation as I APPLY it. More than a surface "pretty," it's a deep down loveliness of Christ that affects my relationships and my reactions, my words, and my works! Read about it in Romans 12:2-21. WOW! That's the glamour we need to grab.

After Katelyn, Autumn, and I had applied our many shades of lipstick, Autumn said, "Now we're pretty, right Gramma?" "Oh yes, and wait till Grandpa sees us. He's going to say, 'Katelyn and Autumn, you're beautiful and I see your mommy in you!'."

My dear sister, all day long we have the opportunity to apply the many colors of God's grace; so by God's grace share your faith with someone, encourage others to be faithful. Your example and enthusiasm is very influential! Even as Katelyn decided to "join in" as she watched Autumn, your actions and attitude will affect others. Look forward to applying godly patience, forgiveness, and kindness. Pray one for another. As God, our Father, sees, He says "You're beautiful, and I see Jesus in you."

13 TWISTIES

Two, little, ever-ready boys charged up and ready to go, burst through my back door and my quiet second cup of coffee. "Grandma, let's do twisties!" "What are twisties?" you ask. In our backyard we have an "adult-sized" swing set (Clint's adult size body broke the child size swings) that is set just beyond the reach of a grand old willow tree. So not only do you swing into the "tentacles" of the nearby willow tree, but IF you are brave enough, I will "twist" your swing as many times as you feel brave, and with a "heave-ho" send you hurling toward the tree, spinning, as well as, flying! If you are feeling "child-like" today I'll do it for you too.

"Okay boys, let Grandma put on her extra-support tennis shoes and we will head for the swings. So how many twisties do you want today?" "Eighty! No, Ninety! No, maybe a hundred!" squeal the boys. "You're kidding, why, you're gonna wear me out!"

"Wear you out, Gramma?" Well, that phrase ("wear me out") tickled Jackson's mind as he spun it though his thinking. With childlike abandon (which is naked truth

without the coverings of diplomacy or graciousness)
Jackson threw his head back with laughter! He shouted,
"Gramma? I'm gonna wear you out!" He felt the power
in that little phrase, and I think his testosterone rose to a
new level. Wil, parroting anything his brother said, joined
in the laughter and asked, "Gramma, can I wear you out
too?" Oh, the squealing and screams that were all part of
the fun!

That little swinging adventure was such a picture of
"life." One minute enjoying a second cup of coffee, and
the next, "life" bursts through our back door, boasting
with the power to "wear me out!" It comes out of the
blue, wraps us in willow tree tentacles, sends us swinging
out of control, but the squeals and screams are NOT
from the "fun" of it.

There are two things you can count on: 1. That second
cup of quietness won't last long, and 2. "Life" will always
burst in and boast about how "powerful" it is. But, more
important than those inevitables, is the truth that I can
ALWAYS count on the Lord, who is my Helper (Psalm
54:4). Hebrews 13:6 promises, "So that we may boldly
say, the Lord is my helper, and I will not fear..." Don't
you just love that word: boldly. I can be bolder than life's
boasting. Someone reading this truth needs to say that
aloud right now, and then LIVE unto that Truth.

Yes, Life, you will wear me out. It's appointed unto me
once to die, according to Hebrews 9:27. You will wear
me out physically, and even support tennis shoes will not
be enough one day. But it is a shallow victory! Why even
today I can do in this life that which will last for eternity.
In all my ways, I can acknowledge Him (Proverbs 3:5). I

can honor Him by making important that which is important to Him. "Faithfulness" is a big deal to my Father. In this full but fleeting Saturday I can lay up treasures for my Tomorrow. So when you wear me out, my soul and spirit will swing higher than it ever has before!

"Higher, Gramma! Higher than I ever have been before!" shouted Wil. There is something deep within us that strains against these shackled bodies. We just can't seem to get "high" enough. Perhaps our souls remember soaring…these "made in His likeness" bodies don't need wings to fly. Jesus ascended without them…In the beginning did Adam and Eve have to put one plodding foot in front of the other? Perhaps not. Remembering the child like desire to go "higher than I've ever been before" I pushed Wil higher, and oh the squeal of delight!

One day soon we are going to ascend HIGHER, higher than we've ever been before…oh the squeals of DELIGHT!

So, if your metaphoric second cup of contentment, if or quietness has just been split by "life" boasting it's going to "wear you out." Nod your head with me in agreement, because it is a truth, it will. But as His children, we LIVE unto a higher Truth, one that sets us free to swing higher than we ever have before. The Lord is my Helper! That is a Fact; therefore, I will not fear. I will live with today's "twisties" in a way that Honors my Father and promotes that which pleases Him.

Now you're just gonna love this verse. Luke 6:35, "But love ye your enemies, and do good, and lend, hoping for nothing again; and your reward shall be great, and ye shall be the children of the…(ready?) Highest." I am a child of the Highest, and He takes me higher than I have ever been! How? Look at the verse, 1. Love your enemies. 2. Do good. 3. Lend not just in terms of money, but in time; prayer support; helping. And the result will be great reward! Delight in being a child of the Highest! So get in your swing and go higher!

14 SATURDAY TO DO

Remember Saturdays when we were kids? Apart from a few child-sized chores, the day stretched out like a delicious, mile long smorgasbord where I could pick and choose just what I wanted. That I could "choose" with friends (usually my sister) made it even better!

Now we've grown up and that buffet or "choice" has shrunk down to the size of a fast food drive thru. More chores than choices.

If my Saturday "To-Do" list already has me sighing, it is my first symptom of not living with God's available grace, which is freely given for this day! It is so easy to look at the "To-Dos" and then experience the consequence of living unto the doing. What are those consequences? They are every feeling from weariness to worrying. Yikes! I hate those feelings; I'm not living full (of God's grace) I'm emptied. I feel like Snow White's Step-Mother, who drank the potion and turned into a witch. As I offer my poison apples (because that is all witches have to offer) it affects everyone around me.

There is one simple (simple, not easy) solution. Learn, learn, learn (practice makes perfect) contentment by "Giving thanks always for all things…" (Ephesians 5:20)! Let's put it into practice right now: Thank you, Father, for legs that can go up and down steps; thank you, Lord, for my car and that it has gas! Thank you, Lord, for hands that can help and hold; thank you, Jesus, for eyes to behold your handiwork; thank you, Father, for the blessing of going to ladies' retreat. Then we must practice thanking Him for things that didn't go our way: thank you, Father, that my children are recovering from the flu; thank you, Lord, for the blessing of staying home with these responsibilities, maybe next year I can go to ladies' retreat. Thank you, Lord, for Your sufficiency, especially while I have shingles (and not the kind that go on the roof)! Lord, you do all things well, and the older I get the more I pray "take over my makeover." I will trust in You.

As I switch my focus to Him (as opposed to my "to do" list or today's disappointment), as I change my words on purpose to thank Him and praise Him, it will accomplish His work in me. First, He opens my eyes to what He is doing. "Consider the lilies, they toil not, neither do they spin…" The Lord is reminding me, "Kathy I will take care of your 'cares.' Trust Me and acknowledge Me in all your ways." Secondly, it quiets the "witch" in me. She talks trash. She complains, gripes, whines, doubts, fears, and lies! Constantly telling me to bite the apple, I have learned the only way to shut her up is by speaking the Truth. God's word is powerful, setting us free.

When Katelyn was younger, she would sit by Grandpa (Pastor), while her mom and dad sang in choir. She had paper and pen, and she was busy "doing, doing." She worked hard and was so proud of her "doing." "Grandpa, Grandpa! Look at my letter (practicing her alphabet "K")." She was so proud of what she could "do." Then she would whispers, "It spells 'I love you'." Now what please Grandpa more? What she could "do" (by the way, it wasn't anything except the letter "K") or what she could "be" (a loving granddaughter)?

My father is so much more pleased with my love and fellowship than merely my efforts (which also are usually misspelled). So, if your day is already filled with sighing or griping, or if there are poison apples of discontentment, know that the antidote is giving thanks for all things. Oh, and get in the right company! God says, "Look at my letter, it spells 'I love you' (and there are no mistakes in His letter)."

15 SWEET SMELLING SAVOR???

According to Ephesians 5:2, what makes me a sweet savor? Sacrifice! The sweet smelling savor comes from the pot simmering over the fire of attitude rather than activity, and of availability rather than ability.

When the Holy Spirit knocks at my door, wishing me to sacrifice, do I give excuses or do I give off a sweet savor? Remember the little boy and his lunch? Never did a fish sandwich smell so good to the nostrils of our Lord!

What else brings sweet aroma to God? Psalm 51:15-19 tells us, "…a broken and contrite heart" is the sacrifice he desires. The focus is placed on being right on the inside before doing right on the outside. If that gets out of order, my life is simply an odor. Considering the Pharisee and Publican (Luke 18:10-14).

In my home do I make the inward sacrifice and forgive, or am I like the Pharisee: judgmental, condemning and full of pride? When an offense occurs rub it out (expunge it, forgive it); don't rub it in.

Sometimes I need a word picture to help me as I battle unforgiveness, so I visualize an old crow! Like an old crow that cannot stay away from road kill, my mind will continually go back and peck at the person or circumstance that I refuse to forgive. Eating off the dead garbage I take on the stench; losing my sweet scent.

Know that the Holy Spirit lives within you and me (as Christians) to assist and promote forgiveness. We can do all things through Christ who strengthens us.

Know that we can choose our thoughts (Philippians 4:8)!

Know that we can be transformed to His likeness (Romans 12:1-2).

Don't try to forgive someone for being what he or she is. Forgive people only for what they do. Forgive in verbs (continual action), not nouns (naming person, places, and things).

Know that forgiveness is never easy! Like surgery, it hurts! But healing can only begin after the infection has been eliminated. Create in me a clean heart, O God, and renew a right spirit within me.

Checklist for becoming a sweet aroma:
(Or how to become an odor-eater)

- ✓ WORDS! WORDS! WORDS! Proverbs 18:21
- ✓ Add value to the people in your life with your words. The average person speaks enough words every day to fill at least twenty pages a day, thirty-six books a year, two thousand three hundred and

ten books in a lifetime of speaking sixty-five years. What best sellers have I written? Practice "pleasantries" in your conversation at home. Be interested in them.

✓ Meet needs in advance: I thought you could use this today (cough drops, Kleenex, chocolate.)

✓ How can I make their life more enjoyable? (When waiting in the restaurant to pass the time, play I spy. Make car time a time to sing fun songs.)

✓ Show enthusiasm toward each member of your family. Find one positive thing every day and express it.

✓ Subtract the junk. Don't major on the mistakes; focus on problem-solving. Mistakes are the opportunities to problem solve together. Address frustration with empathy: "How may I help?" "I'm sorry about this rotten day." "I love you." "I'm praying for you."

✓ Make the mundane mysterious! "Look under your plate." "Whoever says the word I'm thinking of before dinner is over gets out of doing the dishes." Put notes under pillows, in lunches, and pockets. Memorize scripture together, and share how God used His word in your heart that day. Find ways to make today a sweet smelling savor.

16 GIVE AND TAKE

My heart is filled with such sweet contrasts: a week ago I held our newborn grandson – a life given; yesterday we buried a friend and godly deacon in our church – a life taken. The common denominator is both are for God's glory; both are life. What has set me to thinking is that life at some point begins to take more than it gives.

Is your getting out of bed more like a fall and not a leap? Do you find your mailbox filled with more bills than your Facebook is filled with friends? Multitasking has turned into the ONE thing I do. All of us will reach that point. There are some, who like Clint, live with extra challenges; they begin with life taking more than it gives.

Jesus deals with our natural born, grabbing tendencies by giving us instruction: "It is more blessed to give than to receive." What a bitter pill to swallow if in all my ways I acknowledge only me because this life is a taker, not a giver. The antidote is to acknowledge God in all my ways, Proverbs 3:5-6. Do you know how to acknowledge God in your ways? The practiced application of learning to live as a giver is found in Proverbs 3:5-6.

Being filled with all my own ways is the description that God gives of a backslider. God's Word is very clear that this life is short: a vapor! In this life is sorrow and trouble; but praise God, I can daily find new life in Him. If I do not choose to find my life in Him, I will find this life will disappoint me today.

First, I find new life by being born into His family, even as Caleb was just born into our family; Caleb is eating, growing, and gaining weight, that is what we do naturally. God gives us that example to show us what we should be doing spiritually: eating, growing, and gaining weight. No one else can do that for me, not my church, my husband, nor a Sunday school teacher. Just as no one can physically eat for me, spiritual nourishment is my responsibility. The church, God's institution, the teacher, the parent, all of them can be, and should be, a godly example, which stimulate the appetite by word and illustration, but it ultimately has to be me choosing God and asking Him to grow me as I choose to conform myself to Him. Life can never take away what I commit to Him. David said in Psalm 31, "Into Thine hand I commit my spirit: Thou hast redeemed me O God of Truth." He is not talking about dying, He is talking about living! How is your spirit today? Has it already begun to gripe or feel burdened, has today already grabbed something out of your hand? Today can be a demanding, two year old. Stop letting the day rule you. Commit the part of you (your soul and spirit) that is as young as the moment you began, and then commit the part of you that life will take. Life has access to my strength, health, mind, resources, and abilities. Choose to honor God with it…all day! 2 Timothy 1:12, "For I know whom I have believed, and am persuaded that He is able to keep that which I committed, unto Him against that day." What day? The day life begins to take more than it gives. Do not let life make you childish, but let the Lord make you Child-like.

17 A GOOD FIT

God's Word is our pattern for living, but often a pattern does not guarantee a fit. If you sew, you know what I am talking about. I am finishing up a dress I made for Tina. I bought the pattern, cut it out to her size, but guess what? I still had to make adjustments so it would fit her. In the same way, God's Word is the truth for all of us, but if I do not go for personal fittings, God's Word hangs sloppy or crooked; it does not seem to fit me. The pattern and material for life is God's Word, my fitting is my prayer life. A fast or flippant prayer life is revealed when stress rips my seams or trash rips my day. Stress and trials, which are the pins of life, are meant to secure me to my Father. They are my opportunity to exercise my faith and to show others that "my Father doeth all things well," even the things I do not understand. I trust in Him with all my heart and lean not unto mine own understanding, but in all my ways acknowledge Him. He will perfect my "fit" (Proverbs 3:5-6).

Another reason my faith does not fit is because of a perfunctory life. In my prayer, words may form, but there is no passion, no awareness that I am talking to God. The very God who made heaven and earth, and who delights in talking to me! Like the disciples walking and talking with Jesus on the Emmaus Road in Luke 24, their hearts ripped open, like an ill-fitted sleeve that needs reconstruction. Their faith was not fitting at all on that day. But look what was happening in their broken hearts, even though they were not aware of it at the time! That is how powerful it is to talk with God! In verse 32 Scripture reveals, "And they said one to another, Did not our heart burn within us, while He talked with us by the way." This is the first recorded case of "holy heartburn!"

It is that personal fitting to just what my heart needs from my personal God. He is my father, who delights in dressing me in righteousness that fits me in my family, my home, my work, my world, all for His glory. Is your faith feeling sloppy or too tight; is it not a good fit to your circumstances? I promise you, the issue is not with the pattern, but in the personal fitting, which is your prayer life. Whenever we wear something that fits us perfectly, not only does it feel good, but it looks good!

Tina wears a little summer dress that I made for her back in high school and someone always comments, "I love that dress! Where did you get it?" She smiles and says, "My mama made it!" When we wear our faith and it is a perfect fit in our circumstances, people look and wonder where does she get her strength, her joy, her kindness, her forgiveness, her peace? It is such a privilege to smile and say, "My Father made it."

May you wear your perfectly-fitted faith all day today!

18 WALKING IN THE LIGHT

What a gorgeous week of vacation. We lived, totally spoiled, at the condo on Houghton Lake. I think I grew fins, because we lived in the water. Clint didn't want to come home! He loves the swimming pool. Doug and I brought our games down to the pool, and had the luxury of having it to ourselves. We sipped on ice coffee, and I beat him in Farkle (you must play that game!). Let's hear it for the girls! I have to get someone to root for me because Clint always roots for Dad. Full disclosure: he did beat me in 3-13 (these are not "games" they are "tournaments!").

Okay here's the thought I would like you to live with today. What's the first thing you saw when you opened your eyes this morning? Color! You saw everything in living color! And do you know why? Don't say, "God made it that way." Because, of course, He did, but that is to miss the miracle of it! How many primary colors are there? Three, why? Now this is the kjv (Kathy Jackson version), but I believe there are three primary colors (every shade and variation comes from these three) in "reflection" of the Triune God. (I personally believe every detail of creation is a "visual aid" to my "near-sighted" faith.) "Do not the heavens DECLARE the glory of God." So...could the blue represent royalty, red representing the cleansing blood, and yellow the bright glory of God?

Here is a Biblical Truth I can substantiate with Scripture. (Because, that is very important...I love where my imagination takes me, but it is always secondary to the Truth.) I was struck by the "greenness" all around Houghton Lake! On this summer Saturday flip off your flip flops, run your toes through the green grass, lay on your back, and look up at the green foliage in an enormous tree. As you do, consider this: each leaf is like a room; it has a floor and roof supported by thousands of tiny pillars. Inside this room food is manufactured; sunlight filters through the transparent roof above. The floor has up to 100,000 stomata (mouths) per inch that open and close to let in air. Two "guards" stand at each stoma to see that the right amount of oxygen and water enter the room. The pillars are covered with green chemical specks, which we call chlorophyll. The filtered sun strikes the chlorophyll, initiating a chemical reaction called photosynthesis. Carbon and other elements of the air, entering through the stomata, change to starch, sugar, and oil. All of this produces food!

Now consider beyond what we see, but are so use to that we don't see the Creator. It is through the light that the plant's life grows and "eats" and "is." Without the light there is no life! Could it be, that is why we won't need to eat in heaven? We will be in His Light; there will be no hunger! Wow! We will photosynthesize from Him. We can have the pure enjoyment of a dark, dove ice cream bar, because we will have no need of nourishment (I know you are questioning my idea of nourishment.) Why will there be no need of anything? Because we are in the Light! Don't wait till heaven to get the nourishment you need for today. Get in the Light; He is our food source for our hungry and needy soul. 1 John 1:5 tells us, God is light and in Him is no darkness at all. His light brings color into my life. Don't live one grey day after another. Get into His light; it "Photosynthesizes" us! So, do your Saturday homework of "being a kid again" : run barefoot, make shapes out of clouds, but especially be amazed at the colors around you. Understand we see them because colors are being reflected in and through Light! Do others see Christ reflected in your life? Be full because you are walking in the Light, where we are fed.

19 CHRISTMAS LIGHTS

A week of nightly preaching has filled my heart and mind with godly, convicting, and comforting Truth. I am full! It's the month of November! It is synonymous with fullness. My favorite Thanksgiving joke is, what do you get if you cross a turkey with an ostrich? A Thanksgiving bird that buries its head in the mashed potatoes.

Years ago Doug and I were so excited because the girls were coming home from college! We so missed them, and now we were going to have them HOME! (Some of you may be counting the days until Thanksgiving, when you will hug your child. Even with all the technology, nothing compares to their real presence!) Oh, the wait seemed so long. Time seemed to c-r-a-w-l.

My sweet husband said, "Let's celebrate with lights!" When the girls drive in, let's have "home" lit up! I crawled in the crawl space, pulled out every strand of Christmas lights we owned; Doug went to Aco Hardware and bought all their specials. We strung lights

EVERYWHERE: on the back fence, around every tree, up and down the gazebo. We put a lit tree inside the gazebo, icicle lights hung like dripped frosting all around the house, and with all the work our hearts were bubbling over with excitement. "The girls are coming HOME!"

I will never forget the moment when we saw the car lights turn into the driveway; saw their faces light up with seeing Dad, Mom, and Clint surrounded by lights; knowing it was all prepared to celebrate "them."

Our Father, in anticipation of His children coming HOME pronounces, "Let there be LIGHT!" He knows the moment we will come HOME; sometimes the waiting seems so long. In anticipation of God's children coming HOME, He celebrates with LIGHT! Jesus prepares a PLACE; He lights up the sky with a special salvation Light-the star of Bethlehem. He gives us His Word, which is a Light. "Thy Word is a lamp to my feet and a light unto my path" (Psalm 119:105). Before we get HOME, He makes "us" light trough the gift of the Holy Spirit indwelling us. Then He gives us the privilege of letting our LIGHT so shine that men may SEE our good works and glorify our Father in heaven (Matthew 5:16).

Does your Light so shine on this November Saturday? Has your faith dimmed under layers of "stuff" in this life? It is so easy to just "function" because I have forgotten to recognize and celebrate His Presence (2

Peter 1). All the technology of my faith is still a poor substitution for His Touch.

20 LIGHT

Our November frost has glittered and sparkled over our landscape, beautifying and highlighting like an expert hairdresser. I could not see the beauty until the light touched it. When I did see the beauty, it made me say "Wow!" Being a practiced hair highlighter and canvas painter, I know the time and talent it takes to make it happen. I have had my fair share of "Oh, no!" rather than "Wow!"

After the light broke through and I saw God's handiwork, I paused with a reverent thank you! When we see God's work, it puts us in awe. We have to SEE it. This is the daylight savings day; we set our clocks back so we have more light. The Light of the world is Jesus; and we really won't see, until we see Him! The god of this world hath blinded the world's mind...why? "Lest the Light of the glorious gospel should shine unto them" (2 Corinthians 4:4). I so want to have a shiny-glittery Saturday, how about you? See Jesus in everything you do. He is the Light that enables me to see the sparkle.

His Word is a lamp and a light, not only to show me the way, but to show me the sparkle! Just like this morning's frost, it was there way before I saw it. I did not and could not see it until I had light!

Take some light, a truth from God's Word, and shine it.

Improve our space with some Light. Let your words bring some sparkle into someone else's day (especially a family member's day). Glitter your home with apples of gold, because of words fitly spoken. Even if no one says "Wow!" or "Thank you!" your heart will, as the Holy Spirit whispers, "Well done, that was good! I am 'glittering' you on the inside."

21 GIFTS

For whatever gifts, family, abilities, talents, time, strength, or resources God has given you, THANK HIM! Use them for His glory; but do not glory IN the gifts.

If you have lost a gift lately, learn to say, "Thank you, Father; I will glory in You, whether for the gifts you give me, or for the gifts that go away. Use me today for your glory, I will treasure your gladness in my heart (Psalm 4). I have learned to give thanks in all things. I will rest in Your sufficiency as mine evaporates; I will claim Your fullness as my day empties me and my resources; by Your grace and for Your glory alone, I live. Amen."

I hope that this true story brings a smile and remind you of the truth, "if it is not eternal, it is NOT important." Learn to live light.

I needed to reorganize my home! The other day I started out with the cupboards in the kitchen. Actually, my motivation began the night before as I was putting away leftovers and could not find the lid to the container. All these containers and I picked the one that had lost its lid. Back in the parsonage days I had a small kitchen, much less time, and more children; but every container was stored with its lid ON, every appliance was kept with its attachments. I mean, what good is an electric knife with no blades? And why in the last-minute confusion of making gravy, mashing potatoes, putting ice into the glasses, and greeting company do you want to search in the drawer of the Ronco-matic cheese grater that sleeps beside the powdered sugar-stencil makers that are stacked on top of the Tupperware seasonal Jell-O lids! It is always that moment that you see everything EXCEPT the electric knife.

But, when we keep our kitchen organized there is one thing we lose out on. It is that blushing, rushing, heady, anxiety driven feeling that makes you know you are alive! Your head is banging, your pulse is racing, and you know if you weren't alive there is no way you could feel this rotten. So my advice, if you are not feeling alive...get really unorganized, and do not worry, you will not have to work hard at it, it just automatically happens.

Years ago I was showing the girls how to make gravy. We had company coming over; I had a turkey in the oven and a ham in the crock pot. I had just explained to the girls to put the milk and butter in the mixing bowl fifteen minutes before the potatoes, that way the chill is off the ingredients and the potatoes will not cool off so quickly.

Now the gravy: I usually have the packet that I use for a base, but for some unorganized reason I had not checked my cupboards. No problem, I was making gravy before they invented those little packets. Tina got out the chicken bouillon, as I was boiling a cup of water. Next it was time to get the stock. I opened the oven door, pulled the rack out that the turkey roaster was on, and showed them all the good gravy stock on the bottom of the pan. I explained how the top layer of butter (grease) had to be skimmed off. I pulled open the drawer to get my big slotted spoon, the one that sleeps beside Mr. Ronco-matic, and I inadvertently pushed the roaster pan back on the rack without pushing the rack back. When I let go, my rack tipped up! This caused my roaster to tip over, and my turkey to tip out! Well, he didn't actually roll out, my oven wasn't that big, but all the juices spilled out, causing huge, bilious, black cloud formations. Of course, the company was coming over in 25 minutes, and this was grease, so we are talking fire! I quickly turned off the oven and burners, threw open the drawer with the dish towels in it, and beat out the little butter fires that had started on the bottom of my oven. During this time I managed somehow maintain a cool, detached composure. I turn to my astonished daughters, and quietly said, "open the windows and doors: the back door, the front door, the French doors, and the patio doors." Meanwhile, I put a lid on top of Mr. Tom Turkey to keep him hot, the green bean casserole was delegated to the microwave, and I began wiping out grease, butter and turkey stock from my oven. "Hmmm, how can I keep the turkey hot for another 15 minutes?" was the question pulsing through my head. The house was now freezing with everything open; but I wasn't sure I should I dare turn the oven back on. "Did you get all the residue wiped up, Mom?" asked one of the girls. By that point the smoke was filtering out, our eyes were no longer tearing, "Yeah, I think it'll be fine. Let's go for it." Turkey went back in, the oven was turned back on and in just a couple minutes I knew I had made the wrong decision....May Day, May Day! As if rehearsed, we turned off oven, reopened doors and windows, squinted against more billowing smoke, and grabbed more towels to smack out the little fires. "God bless whoever folded laundry last night!" shouted one of the girls. "Okay, plan B, no more oven, capture the last drippings to make gravy, add more chicken stock, turn down burner, keep stirring so the gravy does not congeal, add seasoning, sage, pepper, sprinkle in flour and keep stirring, taste, add some salt...taste, YUM!" the instructions poured forth like the grease had just poured from the pan. I looked at my girls, smiled, high-fived, and said, "And that is how you make homemade gravy!"

We closed the doors and windows; the company was right on time. When they walked into the house they exclaimed how good it smelled! We stood in our family circle, prayed, and people lined up with their plates as Doug carved the bird. When he commented on how it had a different color to it. I smiled and said, "Yes, Dear, this year we smoked the turkey." The girls and I just smiled and winked at each other. Live light!

22 CHANGE

Go outside and find an acorn and look at it with me.
God uses nature to teach us spiritual truths. God wants
to speak to us about change. We too have "changed."
We have changed from being that eight pound baby with
no hair and fat cheeks. What brings about the change?
GROWTH! God made us to grow!

Every child cannot wait to grow. Jackson teases me with
"Grandma, I'm growing!" He knows that it gets the
intense reaction: "Nooo, Jack, you are growing way too
fast!" Autumn tells me that since she is now three, she
can do more big girl stuff. When, I asked her what she
wanted to do, she looked at me and said, "Grandma!
You don't know! I just want to do more big girl stuff."

In childhood all our "doing" became the vehicle that
transported us into "being someone more!" More
powerful, more magical, more beautiful, more
talented…more than "just" me. For a few moments as

we copied and pretended; we became that person; from Cinderella to Rudolf the Red Nosed Reindeer. Then we grow up and no matter how much "big girl" stuff we do or accomplish, it still leaves us feeling empty. The pursuit of doing "more" does not deliver us to the castle but to the dirty cinders. I'm left on the island of misfits.

After reinventing childhood, that childhood being the magical time when you can be and do anything you want, Solomon writes, "It is vanity (empty)!" Ecclesiastes 11:10.

Katelyn wore her princess tiara Wednesday night; it made her "a princess!" Autumn applied lip gloss all over her lips, and proudly said; "There, now I'm Mommy." How sad that so many of God's children continue in the empty patterning of childhood, manipulating the outside to try to be something "more" on the inside. Failing to understand it is the companionship of the Holy Spirit who lives within us that makes us more, more than just "ME."

God places in the soul the yearning to be more, it is trapped in this earth-bound body. Our immortal soul whispers to this mortal baggage, "You were meant to be more." It is the Holy Spirit's miracle of transformation, His enablement to live a supernatural life. It happens on the inside. Romans 12:1-2 instructs, "I beseech you therefore, brethren, by the mercies of God, that ye present your bodies a living sacrifice, holy, acceptable unto God, which is your reasonable service. And be not conformed to this world: but be ye transformed by the renewing of your mind, that ye may prove what is that good, and acceptable and perfect, will of God." He tells me to "copy." We know how, we have been copying since childhood, ever since we made a cape out of a pillowcase and a crown out of tin foil. But instead of copying so that I can be Cinderella, I'm to copy Christ, so I can be like Him. One is make-believe and leaves me empty, and the other is real and makes me grow. As I dress up in His garments of praise (Isaiah 61:3), and as I put on according to Ephesians 4 and Colossians 3, I can know He will do His change in me. Philippians 1:6 says, "Being confident of this very thing, that He which hath begun a good work in you will perform it until the day of Jesus Christ."

So find your acorn, enclose it in your hand and then pray for God to make you more like Him, changing and growing into the one He designed you to be!

23 FIRE

I'm catching a scent of something good! I love the scent of fall. It is amazing to think we can smell a season! No other time of the year has such pungent smells. Early one morning Doug opened the front door to get the paper; he called to me, "Kath! You're gonna love what today smells like! Someone's built a fire!"

The scented air rushed in on cold feet seeking warmth; I breathed deeply, and while the aroma of burnt, wet leaves filled my nose, it was my heart that was affected. Rich, colorful memories fell and twirled from my "tree of life." Nostalgia embraced me.

Do you know what "nostalgia" means? "A wistful desire to return in thought or fact to a former time in one's life; to one's home or homeland or to one's family; a sentimental yearning for the happiness of a former place or time."

Deep within every human being lives and breathes an eternal soul. It is as young as the moment God breathed into man, and man became a living soul. My soul, locked in paradise lost, has the wistful desire to return Home. It yearns for the happiness of a former time. The time it enjoyed the very presence of God, drinking the springs of Living Water. Jesus, and only Jesus, makes it possible for my soul to be saved and once again sit in His presence. John 14:21-23 states, "…and he that loveth me shall be loved of my Father, and I will love him, and manifest myself to him…If a man love me, he will keep my words: and my Father will love him, and we will come unto him, and make our abode (Home) with him."

Jesus built a fire on the beach in John 21. He knew its light and scent would waft across the waves to his discouraged, disillusioned disciples. The scent of fire and fried fish drew them in, but they did not just take on the scent of the fire, they took on the scent of godliness. Their lives became a sweet smelling sacrifice, drawing other yearning souls to the Savior.

Jimmy turned eight years old yesterday; he was in church this past week bubbling over with the excitement of, "It's my birthday, Pastor Dan. Guess what? I had a piece of cake and it was different than any other cake I've ever had! And guess what else? My mom was there!" Walking into church for our Thursday Night Evangelistic Meeting, he bursts out with, "Pastor Dan! I love coming to church…it's not even Sunday and I can come to church!" As he walked in, he asked, "Pastor Dan? Can I leave my coat in your office? It smells like my grandma's smokes."

My heart ached with all he did not have, it hurt to hear his joy over, "My mom was there." What touched me deeply was his childlike faith, his eagerness for God and church. It was not out of guilt: "Well, I better go, or God won't love me." God loves and offers ALL His grace because He is God; God IS love. Nor was his choice self-serving, "I should do this and be that…so my life will turn out the way I want it to…" My, how we "grow-up" narcissistically childish, instead of child-like. The truth of God's love is not based on my behavior.

That soul, under-indulged from life's pantry, even void of the aroma of motherhood, recognized the scent of godliness and raced toward the GOOD. Somehow even child-like faith knows to shed off worldly smells; whether it be a little coat saturated with grandma's cigarettes, or the inward yearning for the wraps of guilt to be unwound and discarded, or the cover up of sin confessed, forgiven, and removed.

A child-like faith breathes in the scent of godliness and follows it to the Savior for the pure joy of sitting in His presence. The nostalgic yearning of the soul whispers, "Home at last." Follow the scent of godliness and by all means let it take you Home.

24 AUTUMN JOY

Do you know Autumn Joy? I'm not talking about the season or an exhilarating response to it. I'm talking about the plant. It's a perennial in the sedum family, and it's called "Autumn Joy."

Autumn Joy! Why, it's mere name flaunts its fearlessness! For most, the season of autumn brings a shiver of coming winter, but not Autumn Joy. "Joy" comes in the morning (Psalm 30:5). There is a "waiting" for it, and it is through the "night." Strapping on the shoes of faith, I will not fear the night, nor the cold, nor the dark, because I know what is coming. "Joy!" comes in the morning. She (the sedum) blushes with the secret of her joy. She flourishes while others fade. Right now my Autumn Joy is an enormous, glorious globe of radiance; she's brilliant while everything else is burnt out. She patiently waits. Colossians 1:11, "Strengthened with all might, according to His glorious power, unto all PATIENCE and long-suffering with JOYFULNESS." Why, anything can flourish in the summer sunshine, but Autumn Joy declares her strength BECAUSE of the cold! What do I declare in my "cold" times? She tosses her well formed head as the cold marches into her garden, her space. All around her other foliage drops, droops, and dries, but not Autumn! Oh, she blushes in the effort, but it only beautifies her image, which reflects her Maker and gives her opportunity to STAND (Ephesians 6:13-14).

If Autumn could talk, she wouldn't; she would shout: "I did it! I survived five sets of running, jumping, carefree grandchildren's feet! I withstood the dog, the raccoons, the squirrels, and even the fox! I grew and flourished despite dry spells and sunless days." And then because all of creation is my Father's visual aid, by which I will clearly see His Eternal power (Romans 1:20), I know Autumn Joy would invite me to join her victory shout and know that I too can be an "Autumn Joy!"

You need to plant this full-proof, hardy perennial. It's such a picture of God's faithfulness and a growing faith. It roots deeply and has a well formed structure; it doesn't randomly encroach in places it shouldn't be. Reminding me, "Kathy, don't live randomly." Don't live randomly in your thoughts: 1 Corinthians 10:5, "…bringing into captivity EVERY thought to the obedience of Christ." Don't live randomly in your words: Psalm 19:14, "Let the words of my mouth be acceptable in Thy sight O Lord…" Don't live randomly in your feelings: Proverbs 4:23, "Keep (guard!) thy heart with all diligence…" It is God's Word that gives "structure" to my naturally random ways. I am prone to wander, just like a weed.

25 GEESE

Are you having as hard a time letting go of summer as I am? So I am choosing to find beauty everywhere I look, and there is plenty to see. The other day there was such a noise in the sky; I looked up in amazement to see the V formation of geese flying south. Being the directionally challenged person that I am, I was so impressed as I watched them travel to a destination they could not see, and some had never been to before. God put that directional sense in them. It tells me I can trust my Father's direction even when I cannot see my destination, and I am heading into territory I have never been to before.

Here are some other interesting facts my sister shared with me. As each bird flaps its wings, it creates an uplift for the bird immediately following. By flying in V formation the whole flock adds at least 71% greater flying range than if each bird flew on its own.
Thought: People who share a common direction can get where they are going more quickly and easily because

they are traveling on the "uplift" from one another. When a goose falls out of formation, it suddenly feels the drag and resistance of trying to go it alone and quickly gets back into formation to take advantage of the lifting power of the bird in front. Thought: Flying outside the will of God will drag me to a place that will be hard and burdensome. I must get back into formation. His yoke is easy and His burden is light – easier and lighter than what? Than the yoke and burden I will carry if I choose to fly my own way.

When the head goose gets tired it rotates back in the wing and another goose flies point. The geese honk from behind to encourage those up front to keep up their speed. Thought: What do we say when we honk from behind? Again, God has given us the right instruction that makes the trip sweet. "A word fitly spoken is like apples of gold in pictures of silver." Hmmm, finally, when a goose gets sick or is wounded by gunshot and falls out of formation, two other geese fall out with that goose and follow it until it is able to fly or until it dies. Only then do they launch out on their own, or with another formation to catch up with their group. Wow! Let's follow the directions God gives us in His Word TODAY. While following His Word won't take me to Florida, it will take me to a blessed space, and there is nothing better than that on this fall day.

26 SHORT CUTS

This weekend marks the end of summer and many of you are aching with "endings" as you hug your college child goodbye or pack that first lunch for your kindergartner. I don't say this flippantly, or in vain repetition, "God Is Faithful." He will fill your emptiness. He is the Author of Fullness. I know this experientially because we girls share our feelings; but more importantly I know this from His Word and Promises, and I share that from Truth!

Morning light was just creeping in when school schedules demanded an earlier "rise and shine!" K-5 grandson, Jackson, leaped into this adventure by waking up at 5:40! That was a full hour before he needs to be up. Tina (mom) heard him and whispered, "Jackson, come lay down by mommy. You need to sleep another hour." Jackson was totally convinced he knew what he needed, but he crawled into bed with his eyes wide open. "Close your eyes, Jackson, you have a big day and we have Wednesday night service tonight. You need your sleep." "But Mom, I have so much energy." In his little mind this completely explained why sleep and energy could not cohabitate in his 5 year old body. "Jackson, if you want to grow big and strong, you have to sleep." "It's okay mom, I'll just take a vitamin pill."

While that was an amusing answer, I find that answer echoed in my own heart. My heart always seeks a short cut: a way that "seemeth" right to me (Proverbs 14:12). After all, every man's way is right in his own eyes (Proverbs 21:2). Well, guess who was so sleepy at school nap time that he couldn't wake up? And then he had to deal with the grogginess and grumpiness that made every task so L-a-b-o-r-i-o-u-s. My heart's short cuts often end up making me spiritually groggy. When I cut out prayer time, explaining to God, I'll just pop in later. Like Jackson popping a vitamin for growth, it just doesn't happen.

When I take the short cut of worrying, which comes so naturally and certainly is easier than trusting, it makes daily tasks so much heavier, as I carry around a heart filled with ache. God says very specifically to be anxious over nothing, but that in EVERYTHING with prayer and thanksgiving to let my requests be made known to Him. With eyes wide open, I explain to God why "fear and faith" cannot cohabitate in this body. He agrees, and asks me to choose Him. My mouth is always seeking a short cut. That quick, cutting or needless remark needs a plan. My heart can condone anything I WANT to say. Then guess what grumpiness does? It devours every good, growing relationship.

God has a Good and Growing plan for His children.
From our time and talents to our mouth and mind. It's
for His glory and His great purpose, but when I take my
short-cut I circumvent His growth in me.

As a lover of history and words, I pass this illustration
on to you. The old gardener in Versailles was in sad
distress! What pains he took with his flowerbeds! He
patiently mapped them all out in the evening and
carefully planned his designs. He longed for summer,
soon he would see the perfect patterns and beautifully,
blended blossoms. But the joy was never his; for as soon
as his rare seed was planted, his delicate plants tenderly
set, the lords and ladies from the palace trampled them
all down and reduced the poor gardener to tears.

Season after season the noble men and ladies in their
strolls among the beautiful terraces and graceful gardens,
thoughtlessly destroyed the cunning labor of the old
man's skillful hands.

He could endure it no longer; he would appeal to the
king. So with much trepidation, he marched into the
presence of Louis XIV and confided all his
disappointment and frustration.

The king was sorry for the old man and ordered little
tablets, "etiquette," to be neatly arranged along the side
of the flower beds, and a state order was issued
commanding all his lords and ladies to walk carefully
within the "etiquette." (Thus he enriched our vocabulary
with a new and significant word.)

The Growth and Joy of my Christianity, consists of carefully walking (Ephesians 5:15- circumspectly) within the ways marked out by the etiquette of God's Word.

From carnality to Christ likeness is a long way. MY carnality shouts, "MY WAY." It tramples where it wants, proclaiming "freedom." From the time Adam and Eve revolted against the etiquette that marked off the one tree, mankind has rebelled against God's way. Mankind resents any "Thou shalts" and "Thou shalt nots." But Galatians 5:1 tells me I am FREE when I stand within God's etiquette. Stand fast therefore in the liberty wherewith Christ hath made us FREE and be not entangled again with the yoke of bondage (the bondage of my short-cut carnality).

Louis the XIV never supposed for a moment that the little tablets would prevent the lords and ladies from trampling the bulbs if they were determined to do so. The tables indicated the "king's pleasure" and that is all etiquette ever does. I can easily imagine that for a month or so, while they were chafing under the new restrictions, and while the precious bulbs were slowly developing, the lords and ladies thought the old gardener a real boor, a nuisance to their freedom. But when their promenade became fringed and blossomed with rare and spectacular color and scents, they blessed the old man for his work!

God's Word states our King's pleasure, and how He would have us walk. So often it is indicative not imperative. God does not protect His flower beds with Force. He makes His way clear, even gives us His Spirit to guide us. He defines rewards and consequences, but if we have our heart set on our own way, a short-cut, there is nothing to prevent us from stepping off the etiquette.

May you have a sweet walk with the Master Gardener today. I suggest studying Ephesians chapters 4-6.

27 LAST

The word "last" is a sad word. I associate it with being last in line; the last one picked; the last place contestant; the last one to supper. It gives the connotation of getting only the leftovers; the last cookie is always smallest and broken. Wow, just thinking on being last is such a downer. It is in such contrast to being "first!!"

Wil and Tina were racing, as Tina pulled ahead, Wil stopped in his tracks and shouted, "No, Mommy, I be first!" I was sitting in Katelyn's driveway as she pulled out her awesome bike that her daddy found at a garage sale. With helmet on, she said, "Ok, Gramma, say go!" I said, "1, 2, 3 – go!" She wheeled around the length of the driveway, and as she came quickly pedaling towards me she shouted, "Say the winner, Gramma!" I proudly announced, "Katelyn Kristina Bonner comes in first place!!!" Well, she went on to do this same routine fifteen times! Why? Because she loved hearing that she came in first! Of course, all the other competitors were imaginary.

We all love being first and not last. Life keeps pushing us
into last place, even as I turn my calendar, I sighed in
response to the last of summer. Well, I want to tell you,
my friends, that on this last summer day, you are first in
Christ! Matthew 19:30 shouts, "…and the last shall be
first." This is how we are first all day long.

1. We know we are loved. Our greatest emotional need is
met in Christ, and do you know why? Because He "first"
loved us!! I John 4:19.

2. All day today, seek ye first the Kingdom of God. Our
purpose in living is accomplished in Christ.

3. Compete in Christ! Strive for the mastery, run the race
that is set before us, use our abilities and talents for His
glory and do it with all our might! According to
Ecclesiastes 9:10, "giving God the glory for all we do."

Regardless of what place I come in, when I do all I do
for His glory and with all my might, knowing in Him we
live and move and have our being, Acts 17:28, I am a
winner. Our satisfaction is sweet! Ecclesiastes 2:24,
'That he should make his soul enjoy the good in his
labor," because "it was from the hand of God"
(Ecclesiastes 3:13).

So on this last Saturday of summer; know that we are
not last!!! We are first, and the last thing we may hear
today, is the trump of God. I Thessalonians 4:16 states,
"with the trump of God; and the dead in Christ shall rise

first." I know, there is that first and last thing again, but do not worry we are going to catch up. "Then we which are alive and remain shall be caught up together to meet the Lord in the air: and so shall we ever be with the Lord. Wherefore comfort one another with these words."

28 OH SUMMERTIME

The 4th of July not only brings us to celebrating America, but it is also a blessed time of celebrating summer! Summertime is the steroid for our senses! Summer tastes good! How many barbecued last week, or went to a barbecue? Doug had the smoker and the barbie going. It drove my sensory smell C-R-A-Z-Y! And what about those spoonfuls of sweet and tangy baked beans, blanketed under crispy fried bacon! The hot and tangy balanced with the sweet and juicy watermelon and strawberries. Summer tastes good.

Summer sounds good! To step out doors in July is to step into a symphony, a cacophony. A cacophony is a mixture of competing sounds. In our back yard there are at least a dozen different birds all vying for center stage and the microphone as they belt out their song. You can't believe the sounds competing for your attention. Add to that, squealing grand children, water balloons being launched from a sling shot, marshmallow races, sparklers sizzling, adults talking, patriotic music blaring,

"…and the rockets' red glare, the bombs bursting in air…" pop cans being opened, coffee perking, it is cacophony that never stops. It only changes as daylight slips into pajamas, the birds stop and the crickets begin. Now the grandchildren's bare feet are content to dangle from Grandpa's lap; the spray can of sunscreen is replaced with the spray of mosquito repellant and it says, "shhhhhh." Still the sounds never quit. Hot flushed cheeks have cooled down to droopy, sleepy eyes. After the fireworks it's almost midnight, and four year old Wil is being tucked into bed, unable to part with his glow sticks strung around his neck and arms, he is still making sounds! You wanna know what his last sound is? "But Mama, does this mean the 4th of July is over? It just can't be over!" Tina's last sound to Wil "Shhh, it's okay Wil, there will be more."

And because we have a gracious, creative, eternal Father, we have more! In John 10:10 Jesus promises that he has come that we might have life and have it more abundantly!

But summer's cacophony has the ability to drown out what's most important. The very gifts of summer can addict me to living on whipped cream choices. I can easily fill life's plate with what is easy and accessible and what feels good to me. But know our children will not know what is truly godly, because God has been cleverly legislated out of our summer day by means of politically correct laws and the laziness of God's people.

The freedom we celebrate happened because our founding fathers chose what was godly, not just good.

Choose purity over political and social opinion, choose freedom over free time.

On purpose, knowing that in themselves in the cacophony of life, they could not choose wisely, they prayed, they tuned their ears to the voice of God for His direction. Do you? Do I? Am I aware that every day I need His direction? I won't naturally choose the right way.

Our founding fathers knelt and prayed for wisdom. They were not celebrating; they were constructing a seventeen page document, known as the Constitution of the United States of America! The year was 1787, what were the sounds in their summer life? Church bells, a call to worship, and a call to arms, bugles, drums, prayer meeting, a pledging to America echoed across the hills. "I pledge allegiance to the flag of the United States of America and to the Republic for which it stands, one nation under God, indivisible with liberty and justice for all!" One nation! Where? Under God, under His authority!

The summer sounds that filled our founding fathers' lives were very different from the summer sounds of our week. Will we find the fact that we have so many delightful choices become the fetters that bind us into spiritual slavery?

Satan whispers, "You can't make a difference." Who are we listening to? With the cacophony of opinion you have to know who to tune in. It is a choice, and the truth is God's Word. It says when I choose Him, "We" make a majority. It's not time to give up; it is time to speak up!

Every time I open a paper or hear the news, I am tempted to become overwhelmed with the lack of righteousness and the wave of wickedness.

I pray for America: "May God continue to shed His grace on thee, and crown thy good with brotherhood from sea to shining sea." But God can only preserve America as Christians choose to be salt rather than sugar. Salt preserves. America's preservation is based upon the saltiness of God's people; ye are the salt of the earth.

29 SPIDER

"The itsy, bitsy spider…" The spider lives every day building her home no matter how many times the hard bristles of my broom knock it down; she re-builds! She is resilient, faithful to her purpose, and never quits. As long as she has one of those spindly legs that will work, she will pull herself up to rebuild a new web!

What's my response when the hard bristles of life knock me down? "Really! Again?" Do you know what that prefix "re" means? It means something had been "made," but then because it was ruined, spoiled, or broken it needed to be "made-again." Made again as in: recycled; reinvented; renewed; refreshed; rebuilt; the best one…redeemed!

When you and I refuse to be renewed in Christ in response to the hardness in life, we are ruined, wasted. Exodus 1:14 explains, "…and they made their lives bitter with hard bondage…" How were they made bitter? It was hard bondage, a hard place, living with hard people, every day hard, just like the day before.

Are you living in a hard time today? Perhaps, you are dealing with hard people, or wrestling with something hard to understand? Satan loves to make God's children bitter from hardship. Our bondage becomes the hard thing that hardens and embitters me.

As a church we are grieving over a hard thing to understand. Today, our newest baby born into our membership is in heaven. We will see him soon, but oh the pain in between; the hard, hard place for the parents and the grandparents.

Monday, Tuesday, and Wednesday, living in a state of prayer; praying for God's miracle. God performed it, in His way. Wednesday, my burdened heart became a broken heart. My heart whispered, "Father, I don't understand…" His word replied, "lean not on your own understanding…" My heart wasn't assimilating His Truth. I grabbed a dictionary and looked up the word "lean." Webster says, "To incline or bend (so, it is a direction in which I will go); to rest against something for support; to depend or rely on." Don't rest upon your opinion, feeling, reasoning, for your support, Kathy! It won't hold you! Lean on Me; acknowledge Me in all your ways and I will direct you. I will put your thinking, your response in the way they should go, for My glory. Getting back to my purpose, Isaiah 43:7 says, "Everyone that is called by my name: for I have created him for my glory, I have formed him yea, I have made him."

And so like the spider, regardless of what is broken, I return to my purpose; I begin restringing one Truth to the next; weaving His pattern into my mind, "Let this mind be in you which was also in Christ Jesus"

(Philippians 2:5). To the One who heals broken hearts and makes all thing New; the One who brings beauty from ashes, "…that He might be glorified" (Isaiah 61:3).

The parents write, "Our sweet baby is now a little angel in heaven. We are so at peace about it and we are rejoicing that his body is no longer sick. We know his little life has touched many, and we are so thankful that God chose us to be his mommy and daddy. We love you."

30 BUGS

What bugs you? Some of you are thinking, "What doesn't?" I've got a lot of stuff bugging me. It even bugs me that my mind is filled with so much stuff that bugs me!

Does your day sting with the bug bites of life? We flew home from Nevada last week. I brought a laryngitis bug back with me. It made friends with my sinuses and morphed into some other bug. Grandson, Jackson, had his tonsils removed on Monday. The surgery went fine (Praise the Lord), but there was pain and the process of healing; a fragileness, a sadness. It so bugs me when I feel helpless. Tina swung on the motherhood pendulum of keeping him still as he felt better to comforting and entertaining him as he felt worse. Granddaughter, Katelyn started running a fever last Sunday morning, it rose to one hundred and four. That goes way beyond bugging me. Daughter, Trina woke up Wednesday with a fever and aches. Grandson, Caleb is dealing with natural fussiness of teething; I'm sure it bugs him. Son,

89

Clint is into the fourth week of inflamed tendons, which bugs both of us: ice packs, stretching, exercises, new inserts, and progress at a snail's pace.

The ant can lift and carry more than fifty times their own weight. Well, the weight of my mind and heart feels fifty times heavier with the cares and burdens of family and church family. Then there's the burden of the unsaved world! The will of our Father is that all should be saved! I'm burdened. Paul agrees in 2 Corinthians 4:8-9, "We are troubled on every side! Yet not distressed; we are perplexed, but not in despair; persecuted, but not forsaken; cast down but not destroyed."

We all understand the "troubled" part of that verse, but how do we live the "not distressed" part? Paul gives the instruction in Philippians 4:6, concerning the cares of life LEARN TO PRAY! In everything!

I think it is appropriate we look at the bug that looks like it is praying, the praying mantis. But it doesn't "pray" it "preys!" It has a pious posture, but it is only an appearance of piety. This insect is not only a predator, the reproductive process is marked by cannibalism of the male by the hungry female. Yikes! Let all the insect world be warned "looks can be deceiving!"

Yet how often do we settle for a "form," a "posture," of Christianity, which leaves us living without power. I eat myself up (cannibalism) with worry, fear, anger. Praise God, we have a choice! A developed prayer life opens my eyes to see the lost, and God given opportunities to witness. A developed prayer life secures me in the truth of 2 Peter 1. He has given me all things for life and godliness. I am a partaker of His divine nature. It is in my prayer life that my Father speaks to me His truth from Isaiah 41:13, "For I the Lord thy God will hold thy right hand, saying unto thee, Fear not, I will help thee."

Commit with me to PRAY. It keeps me in the right company, and it keeps me from the hypocrisy of religion. Beware of being a praying mantis.

One last bug fact. Houseflies find sugar with their feet, which are ten million times more sensitive than the human tongue. With my love for sugar, I am so thankful I don't have fly feet.

31 BROKEN

Bringing your broken stuff to the Lord is a personal act of building your faith. When the children were little, all three played long and hard, and on any given day things would get broken. But their Daddy was the superglue king, and he could make it like new. So, when something broke there were tears, but it always ended with, "Daddy fix it! It will be okay; Daddy fix it."

We had a designated corner where we put the broken things. We had our very own island of misfits. When the broken toy was placed there the children were free to go do the important things they needed to do in the rest of their day, which was to play some more. They were not burdened down with the broken stuff because "Daddy fix it."

God wants us to find that same truth and develop that same trust with our broken stuff. There is a designated place where it has to go, or we will keep dragging it around with us and living unto it. Put it where it belongs, Matthew 11:29 says, "Take my yoke upon you and learn of me for I am meek and lowly in heart and ye shall find rest unto your souls. For my yoke is easy, and my burden is light." Psalm 55:22 says, "Cast thy burden upon the Lord and he shall sustain thee." Psalm 61:2 says, "When my heart is overwhelmed lead me to the rock that is higher than I."

Now Satan wants to keep you trapped in the tears and the blaming every day. The truth says, find forgiveness, and extend forgiveness. Your Fathers says, "Leave the broken stuff with me and be free to get up and do the important stuff I have for you today. I am your Father; I will fix it. Matter of fact, as you glorify Me in it, I will use this very broken thing for my glory. You will be salt and light because of it."

32 LINES

It is the last Saturday of June. The air is filled with scents <ah-choo> and sounds of itself; one of my favorite sounds is the lapping of waves upon the beach. Today the water rushes up to "high-five" the beach, and the gentle slap mingles with the laughter of Katelyn and Autumn as they run from the chasing waves that tickle their toes. The heart beat is heard in the rhythmic swooshing of each wave that rushes in only to run back to the lake. It "gives," but it "takes" back.

Each wave seems to be in such a hurry to get to shore. I can relate; can you? Like grandchildren rushing to grow-up; they are running, somewhere, anywhere, just as long as it takes them to doing and seeing and being where they have never been before. Trekking into new territory and taking others with them. "Clint," shouts Jack and Wil, "go on the water slide with us!" "This is how you can go even faster," Jack explains, as he pulls goggles down, pus his hands on the overhead bar to give more torque, and throws himself into the thrill of the ride.

"Come on, Clint; you can do it," encourages Wil. And so he does. I am sure his heart was high-fivin' in his chest!

Another interesting microcosm found in this watery wonder of the wave is it "take-back" after it "gives." Like a mischievous imp, offering its "all", only to grab back and run away. But the wave does leave us with something; its pattern is left. Katelyn, Autumn and I trace the water's lacey line with our fingers; we follow the line (the pattern) the wave left.

"Let's run Grandma, lets follow the lines the waves left before they disappears or another wave covers it."

The Apostle Paul echoes the urgency, "Let us run with patience," Hebrews 12:1. The way we run leaves a line that others follow. As your day races up and falls back, and sometimes falls apart, what pattern does it make? Little fingers and feet are tracing and following it.

Paul instructs in Hebrews 12:13, "And make straight paths for your feet, lest that which is lame (young, immature, unable to walk) be turned out of the way; but let it rather be healed." Very quickly the wave is gone, but the evidence lingers in the line, which it left. Did my line lead to the One, whom even the winds and waves obey (Matthew 8:26) ? Did my line bring healing?

It is the One who drew a line in the sand and declared: "I am the Way the Truth and the Life…" This life quickly grabs back all it seemingly gives, but the finger of God traces two lines that form a cross, and He asks, "Will you follow these lines (Matthew 16:24-25) ?"

His line will lead you to worship, to Sunday school, and to church. Now the wiliness of the wave sings, "It's a glorious summer Sunday" but the wisdom of the Word states, "It's Sunday; O Glory in Me."

His line, which always leads to the cross, will also lead us Home.

Katelyn, Autumn, Caleb, and I filled our pockets with treasures from the beach, but someday, "stepping on shore and finding it heaven," will be the greatest treasure. Then we will know the Life that never takes but only gives. Revelation 22:17 teaches, "And let him that is athirst come. And whosoever will, let him take the water of life freely."

Make a line today that will make a difference for tomorrow; it's the only way to enjoy the waves.

33 CAN'T

The beautiful mantle of June is filled with sunshine, the song of birds, and a certain bug…the June-bug! I love waking up to the sound of a June rain, and I want to talk to you about the June-bug. June-bugs have one good trait: they are small. Can you imagine a 5 pound June-bug getting tangled in your hair? Thankfully those nasty, hard encrusted, directionally challenged, lovers of darkness, eaters of all that is good and green, are small.

Here is an even smaller insect, the ant! There are two things I want you to think about today. Number one, the ant never says "can't," and number two, the ant has a plan. The plan turns "can'ts" into "cans"! I love this. Our Father created the ant to demonstrate his sufficiency. Through a little insect He proves to me that if He cares for an ant, of course He will do this for me. I am His child!

Think about the "can't." Some of you already announced to the world, your flesh, and the devil, that you "can't!" The mumbling words spilled out: "I CAN'T get up; I

CAN'T believe what I have to do; I CAN'T have…" It is just so natural (carnal) to speak what is natural.

Do you know the ant can lift twenty times its weight! It does not look at something "huge" and say "I can't (whimper…whine)." It lives the plan and accomplishes, "I CAN!" I can't wait to give you a plan that begins with taking my eyes off "self" and acknowledges my Savior. "Self" is a horrible task master. It is never satisfied, is always comparing, is keeping me entrapped in the land of "can't."

My son Clint was born with Down syndrome. At nine years old Clint's idyllic life took a different turn. Our last school class of the day was after lunch and recess and that was when something strange began to happen. As I pulled out the last papers we would work on, Clint would just put his arms on his desk and his face into his arms and begin to cry. Clint never cried unless he was hurt physically! It shocked me! "What's wrong, Clint? Does your stomach hurt?" (His friends always shared their cookies with him.) "Did you fall at recess? Are you bleeding!" He would not lift his face; he would just shake his head and keep crying. He would only say one word, and I finally figured out what word he was saying. It was, "can't…can't…can't." Well, this happened for three days in a row, and it was always after recess. Something must have been happening at recess! So the next day I stood at the corner of the building to quietly observe what was "happening."

Clint's classmates were wonderful to him; he had a pazillion friends, but Clint, for the first time was realizing he could not do what his friends did. He could not run fast, he was always last, he could not catch the ball or kick it very far. He could not pump his swing high into the air, he could not connect the bat to the ball. In a world where everybody else could, all Clint saw was that he could not. It broke his little heart; and it broke mine too.

Does God ever, ever make a mistake? NEVER! He does all things well according to 2 Peter 1. Every part of Clint was numbered and named according to God's plan for Clint's life and for God's glory. He equips us for all we need for life and godliness. He gives to EVERYONE a measure of talent and ability. It is up to us to discover it, (and to help our children find theirs) develop it, and use it for His glory.

When all I see is what I "can't" do, "can't" be, or "can't" have, I am like the unprofitable servant of Matthew 25. This servant hid his talent. Why? The Master would have doubled his talent as He doubled the others' talents. But the unprofitable servant looked around and compared what he had to others. Looking around and comparing is always the precursor to saying "I can't." "I don't have what they have," he griped. "I can't __ like they can." So he wasted and buried what he had been given. Just like Clint buried his head in his arms, when we compare it not only takes us to a place of tears, but we also become blind to all that we do have.

I wish you could see Clint today; he would just make you smile. You should see him shoot three pointers; he CAN!! You should hear him quote Scripture and preach; he CAN! You should hear him pray; he CAN! You should see him do his jobs at home and at church; he CAN! You should see him be a great uncle; he CAN!

Ladies, when we begin our day without a plan, letting what comes "natural" just happen...the "can'ts" begin to tumble out like toys crammed into the grandkids toy cupboard. It is a mess! God's plan is a plan that allows me to escape from, "I can't," which is sinking sand to that Truthful place of Solid ground that shouts, "I can do ALL things through CHRIST who strengthens me!"

34 LIGHTNING BUG

How appropriate to have all this gorgeous summer light! In the study of the lightening bug, we find that the lightening bug is the most efficient light in creation. It uses 100% of its energy as "light." Compare that to incandescent light which produces only 10% light while the rest of the energy is heat. God calls His children to be light in this dark world. Am I effective like the lightening bug, or do I just give off heat?

God's Word sheds light on the problem and gives light for the solution. I John 1:7-8 teaches, "But if we walk in the light as He is in the light, we have fellowship one with another, and the blood of Jesus Christ cleanseth us from all sin. If we say we have no sin, we deceive ourselves and the truth is not in us." God's Word is a lamp and a light to my heart and will reveal sin for the purpose of restored fellowship and spiritual growth, which is always my Father's desire for me.

Sin dims my light and stunts my growth, which is Satan's goal. Here is the solution for a dim, small faith. Identify the problem! We are liars, and my lying keeps me deceived about "me" and my faith. I lie to protect me, please me, or promote me; and I choose to believe the lie which keeps me entangled in the sin.

Do you know what a tar baby is? It is a sticky thought, and the more you play with it, think on it, and embrace it, the more bound to it you will be. With every continued thought we will apply another wad of tar, developing a tar baby, which will eventually "stick" me to it (James 1:13-15). My lies to myself and others are my inadequate coverings, like Eve's apron of leaves, of the tar baby within.

Lying comes early, comes naturally and comes easy. When I was about seven years old, my grandparents came for a visit. They brought Florida grapefruit, hugs, kisses, and best of all a shiny silver dollar for each grandchild! Wow! I never had one of those; I had never even seen one.

My younger sister, Krisy, and I carefully placed our silver dollars on our dresser. As Krisy left, I looked at her dollar. Hmmmm, it was shiny and new, and mine was grimy and old. I began building my own tar baby. "I'm not really stealing; I'm just exchanging." Then I began with all the "reasons" I should have the shiny one. "I AM the oldest sister; she won't care; she won't even notice; I deserve this one." I believed those lies because I wanted something that was not mine. But I got even worse! With the tar baby within, I started justifying my actions by finding fault with all of hers! "Mooommm, Krisy's buggin' me; Mooommm, Krisy keeps copying me." I went on to establish my rights as the older sister, just because I wanted something that was not mine.

Think about Satan, the father of lies. How did he fall from his elevated position of the most talented and beautiful angel? He wanted something that was not his, he wanted God's position. Think how differently things would have been if he would have fought the deceit with the truth rather than accepting a lie and another lie and another lie. He could have had a way to escape. God provides a way to escape every temptation with His Word and His Faithfulness (I Cor. 10:13). Satan chose deceit and vainly supported it with lies. Satan's tar baby will turn all nations into Hell as he persuades them to forget God.

I wanted Krisy's silver dollar, and so I lied to myself. I knew I would not get caught, and I took what I wanted without even recognizing what I had lost. Like Esau lifting the bowl of pottage to his lips, it tasted so good, for a moment. I did not know the value that the old, dirty 1899 silver dollar had.

Years later as a young teen making a commitment to Christ, one of the first things the Holy Spirit convicted me of was that silver dollar in my jewelry box. Taking it out, I told Krisy what I had done, and also of the greater value of her 1899 silver dollar that used to be mine! Do you know what? She wanted to give the older silver dollar back to me; she did not even care about it. She just valued our friendship. I kept the shiny one; I needed the cleansing that came not just in forgiveness, but also in restitution. A couple years ago she presented me with a little glitter bag, and the silver dollar was tucked inside; we hugged and laughed.

At the point when I confessed to Krisy, our relationship which was already good blossomed into a deep eternal sisterhood that is a forever, eternal gift because I got honest through the Light of God's Word! Do you know God so willingly forgives (I John 1:9). He does not even want our "trinkets" that we trade off for His friendship; He just wants us, our fellowship. That cannot happen until I get honest about my sin. Then, and only then, will my light begin to so shine!

On this bright, shiny day is your faith dull? Is your friendship strained or distant? Like David, ask God to "search your heart and see if there be any wicked way." His light will reveal it for the sweet purpose of restoring us back into the Light and His fellowship.

35 LIVE LARGE

Taste the sweetness of this God-made summer day like a child! It is how we are to live every day, but somehow we grow up and grow out of that wonder; you know, that "WOW!"

I am seeing that "wow" in living colors as five little grandchildren race out the patio door to the swings and slide under the willow tree. "Come on, Grandma, I wanna race!" Twirling and spinning, arms outstretched, faces like flowers turned to the sun, I watch as they lose themselves in the enormous growth of nature. Bee balm and Solomon's seal hide their crouching bodies. "Come find me, Grandma!" Sun drops are waist high, hydrangeas' heavy heads touch noses, and giggles erupt. Katelyn shows Jackson how a petunia "hugs" your nose when you sniff it in. Autumn perches on a cement toad stool and poses as a butterfly. Fox glove is worn on a finger, and with a little imagination the finger becomes a fairy in flight. Wil and Caleb hide behind an enormous tree trunk.

While swinging high into the waving tentacles of the "octopus" willow tree, Autumn and Wil sword fight the branches. "We're flying like Peter Pan!" The sprinkler becomes a lagoon. It sprays its rainbow colored waterfall and they lose themselves in the sensation of simple delights.

Outsized by everything around them, they live LARGER because they are small. Hmmm. Is that the secret that I have lost? The marvel of childhood isn't a mystery; it's a measurement!

I remember standing at the edge of the Grand Canyon; it swallowed me up. In the landscape of the great ravine I became microscopic, less than a pebble, too tiny to even cast a shadow. My response: "Wow," whispered in reverence to the awe I felt. No wonder God calls me to become a "child" in salvation and in the gift of living my faith. As a child my "wow" never wears out. I felt so small as I stood next to something so great! Its greatness compared to "me" made me feel awe. Focusing less on self and focusing more on something else brings profit into my life. Jesus taught this equation in every gospel. Lose yourself. "...whosoever shall lose his life for my sake, the same shall save it" (Luke 9:24). Making self small is the first step in making today LARGE.

In Matthew 10:39 notice the words, "for My sake." Step into the presence of the One, whom the universe cannot contain (I Kings 8:27)! Start naming who He is and what He does! Point to it. Declare it!

Making a bee-line to the bird feeder, a cardinal flashed by Wil. Amazed, Wil called out, "Brodder! I see a cardinal, a cardinal, brodder...look!" His day is LARGER as he "names" his delight and shares it with someone else.

Oh how easy it is to name my jobs, my responsibilities, my cares, burdens, pains and problems. The wrong "stuff" gets "named," made BIG. I stand in its SHADOW and instead of whispering, "wow," I whine, "woe is me," and my day dulls and shrinks.

I remember Wil "naming" his delights, and the Holy Spirit reminds me to "count" my many blessings. I begin to name them beginning with Him! My God is an Awesome God! Psalm 145 provides the example, "I will extol Thee my God, O King: and I will bless thy name for ever and ever. Every day I will bless Thee; and I will praise thy name for ever and ever...Great is the Lord and greatly to be praised and His greatness is unsearchable!" I will call out! "One generation shall praise thy works to another and declare thy might acts."

Amazingly, I find Life again in the SHADOW of His wing (Psalm 63:7). I whisper "wow!"

36 MEMORIAL DAY

Did your day begin with, "What should I do today?" "What project needs to be started or finished?" "After my responsibilities and duties are done, I'm gonna do…" Wow! Have you thought about the privilege of "choice"? I get to choose today because of those who chose to protect my freedom. Freedom births "choices." Tyranny and slavery buries "choices." I can choose to fish today because others chose to fight yesterday. I have freedom!

We enjoyed a really fun choice the other day. We took the grandchildren to Faber's flower nursery. For all children under ten, they have a free hands-on planting experience. First there is the choice of picking out any four-pack of flowers! Can you picture four children four years old and under getting to pick out any four-pack of flowers! Talk about the privilege of choice! (Dare I say, the pain of choice) So they all made their choice, and then got to go to a potting bench filled with rich, dark soil. There they had their choice of buckets. Thankfully, there were only two color choices: blue or red pails complete with shovels. The boys chose blue, of course;

and the girls chose red. Then we filled the buckets with soil as the owner, John, showed how to dig a hole with their fingers and plant their four beautiful flowers! Wow! They were so proud!

Later that night, Doug, Clint, and I worked on our garden. I planted multiple pots, window boxes, and borders. At 9:30 p.m., I put on decaf and declared "curfew." I love that time at night; it's magical. We looked at the fruit of our labor, choosing not to look at all that still needed to be done. We rejoiced in the choices we accomplished.

With all the freedom of choices that day and with all the expensive flowers, guess which flower pot pleased my heart the most? My huge pots on our deck look professional, but the pot of my heart, my favorite, was the pot held in each grandchild's hand. Hands down, their pots win! Why? Because I value "them: grandchildren." It's the "person" not the pot that held the value! We all worked on those little pots together. I shared in the choices of those little hands as they chose and dug, and planted, and were so proud of their work!

So it is with our Father! He has done such great and marvelous work! Look at what He has planted and potted. But oh, His favorite is the shared work with and through His children! That is what builds a relationship and friendship. Isaiah 41:13 declares, "For I the Lord thy God will hold thy right hand, saying unto thee, Fear not; I will help thee!" Don't worry about that dirt or dropping that pail. Let's pick it up and fix it together! I'm here to help you, grow you, and love you.

Tina made us a story time book; it was much like a golden book of yesteryear. It is entitled, "One Big Adventure Day with Grandpa and Grandma." Included in this book was a special event with emergency vehicles at our school. The helicopter landed in the soccer field and the ambulance and emergency vehicles were there! The book is filled with the grandkids riding and sitting and climbing. There are pictures from our trip to Tim Horton's for sprinkled donuts! Guess what book they choose to "read"? The one they are in, and all the fun memories of being "together!" Do you know our Father is so thrilled over our time together he records it in a book?!

Our Father paid a great price so we could enjoy CHOICES today. We are free in Him. He redeemed me from the slavery of sin and that which would destroy me. I have the privilege of choosing Him amidst the myriad of good choices; I can choose God! And the book He makes is filled with pictures of me. Malachi 3:16 says, "Then they that feared the Lord spake often to one another and the Lord hearkened, and heard it." The "book of remembrance," like my very own golden book, was written before Him for them that feared the Lord and that thought upon His name. Think on that, my very thoughts are so precious to God! Someday soon He will open the books, and I know which one I will pick. It will be the one that shows us together, memories made because of the freedom He gave me and the choice I made.

With all the choices you get to make, will you choose the best? Will you remember the price that was paid so that today you and I can choose? Sunday is still the first day of the week, even though America has chosen to turn it into the "week-end." Make the best choice and get to a good Bible preaching church on Sunday. Our Father wants us to remember and choose Him.

37 WHO?

So, I open my eyes to this new, spring day, and immediately the door to my mind flings open to demands, choices and responsibilities. Who am I going to be?

Early this morning my five year old granddaughter Autumn flings open her bedroom door, "It's Averi's birthday party (her responsibility) and I'm gonna BE Snow White!" I'm thinking along with you, "I wish MY Saturday included a party." So far all I've done is deal with stuff that doesn't work, or is broken, or doesn't feel well. But I still get to choose who I'm going to be. The Holy Spirit convicts me, "Be like Christ." Your frustrations are your opportunity to dress in garments of praise. Even as Autumn puts on her Snow White dress and "becomes" someone else, you put on the garments of thankfulness and become someone else! You'll become Christ-like!

38 SWALLOWED

Yes, it is March, but the weather man said, "Three more inches of snow!" I recently saw a cartoon of a beautiful silver wolf; snow was swirling all around the fine, ferocious animal, almost obscuring him, except for his eyes…they were a bright burning yellow, bespeaking of the fire within. The caption read: "The ground hog said, six more weeks of winter." The footnote read: "So I ate him!"

Don't you love it! Don't you wish you could just eat up everything that bothered you? Well, we can't, but look at what we have in Christ. 1 Corinthians 15:54 tells us, "Death is swallowed up in victory." The enemy of our soul with eyes reflecting the fire of hell, laughs and says, "I'll devour you." So our Jesus blocks the path by dying on the cross and arising from the tomb. My Savior shouts victoriously: "You've already been SWALLOWED!"

39 SPARKLE

If we were kids we would already be out in the snow!
The sparkle mesmerized us; the snow-sirens sang their
alluring song, "Come and Play!" Remember building
forts, pulling saucers, making snow angels, playing pie
tag, can't you just taste the snow on your mitten? Never
was anything so thirst-quenching. Finally, only because
mom was calling, "lunch time," would we peel off our
snow packed layers and come inside. The smell of
tomato soup and grilled cheese would great us at the
kitchen. Yummm! Life was good, all because of the
"sparkle!"

Okay sisterhood of wives, look down at your ring finger
and see the "sparkle." Does it reflect what is in your day?
Am I making "sparkle" in my home? Can I find
"sparkle" in my home? I am not referring to the layer of
dust, but rather the level of delight. This is the Saturday
before Valentine's Day; life can so quickly smudge the
"sparkle." Some of you are saying, "smudge" nothing;
why there's not a glint, nor a shimmer! I need more than
a sparkle, I need a miracle! Hmm, I always smile when I
think about the fact that Jesus performed His first

miracle at a wedding. That marriage started off needing a miracle.

After our wedding day comes the dailiness of life. Add to that emotional, spiritual, physical, financial struggle, and it is no wonder we wonder where the wonder went. So, let me shout it out…we have a wonderful Father who has provided "…all things for life and godliness" (2 Peter 1:3). That includes "sparkle!" If you do not believe me, look out at the snow as His Light shines on it. Look at the summer rose as the dew drops from the petals. If God has a "sparkle" for all of that, in every season, don't you know that He has "sparkle" for you!

Often "sparkle" is not found in the obvious places. Matter of fact, the obvious sparkle many times is a counterfeit sparkle. Just ask Judas, the glitter of gold did not bring sparkle; it brought death. Ask Samson, as he kissed the shimmering lips of Delilah. It did not sparkle; it brought enslavement and death.

In the dailiness of marriage, it is so easy to chase a counterfeit sparkle. Too busy, too distracted, too tired, too hurt, too whatever and the wedding of Cinderella has evaporated and morphed into Cruella de Vil. Yikes! How did that happen? Look to your Father who designed a perfect plan for "sparkle." God's "sparkle" is often found in the tear that runs down your cheek. It makes me ready for His miracle. He provides the thirst quenching Water that lasts longer than the snow on the mitten. He fills us with spiritual nutrients that are more satisfying than tomato soup and grilled cheese. Even now He is calling you in for lunch, "Come and dine!" Every day our need to be reminded of God's plan that praises and promotes the "sparkle." "Seek and ye shall find" (Matthew 7:7).

40 BOX UP CHRISTMAS

How many of you have packed up Christmas? Every strand of lights, the wreaths and bulbs, the manger scenes and tinsel, is it gone?

My four year old grandson, Jackson, came down stairs from his nap as his mom was packing up the last few ornaments off the tree. With a shocked, tearful plea he said, "Mama, you just can't box up Christmas!" Every time I "box up" Christmas I feel the same way. As I hold the bulbs, I am trying to hold on to the moments. I can just "see and hear" Katelyn and Autumn jumping and squealing. Oh, you should see Autumn's dark curls bounce when she jumps as Grandpa declares, "Let's do Christmas now!"

There is something about the "endings" that bother us. Oh, we learn to subdue it. As the Christmas season ends, the year pours itself out and the world pours itself a drink, that is how they subdue it. If the reveling and partying is loud enough, the whisper of the soul that lives inside every human being won't be heard.

Do you know what the soul whispers every day? If you don't, it is only because you are not listening. Let me mentions some times when you and I were more apt to hear it. Your soul whispered at your last birthday, especially if it was a decade turner. We heard it when we graduated and went off to college; heard it when our baby had a baby; heard it when we buried a parent or a friend. The Spirit whispers its truth every day. Do you want to know what it is saying? "You are an immortal soul." You see, your soul is eternal; it is forever; it has no ending. My flesh, "this outward" me, deals with "endings" all the time. I used to have fresh, smooth skin; I use to multitask efficiently. My soul is a juxtaposition. When the temporal touches the eternal, the soul whispers, "See, I told you. It is not going to last, it has to end, it is over, it is done." Like a soft skinned orange feels the cut of the grater, our eternality feels the cut of our temporal, and it grates.

We hold the Christmas decoration, the $2.00 bulb that represents priceless moments, and we too plead with the words of Jackson, "don't box up Christmas!" Has it ended already? While the truth of the soul whispers, "yes." If we look to the truth of the One who makes us eternal, we will hear, "So teach us to number our days that we may apply our hearts unto wisdom." You see there is something we can do; it is our choice to apply God's wisdom. Even as you apply ointment to a cut for healing and wellness; God has an ointment that we may apply to this juxtaposition for healing and wellness. Most of our earthly endings are God given primers meant to get our attention and reveal our need for His Presence, His Eternality, and His Forgiveness. As I apply His truth to my day and do all I do for His glory, He makes that moment eternal!

41 NIGHT LIGHT

Late one night, Clint walked into our room with his night light. "Father, it doesn't work." "Ok, Son, I'll fix it in the morning," Doug replied. I added, "Clint, the light from your vaporizer is on-that gives light in your room." All was quiet, but Clint was still standing there. "What's wrong?" Doug asked. Clint again responded, "My light doesn't work." Doug flipped back the covers, went to the hall closet, got a new bulb, screwed it in, connected it to the outlet, and "there was light!" All was well. Doug came back to bed; now we could all sleep. But "lo" behold at the end of our bed stands, not a Christmas angel, but Clint (my own angel) holding up his other night light! You see, Clint had two night lights, and you can guess what his next line was..."Father, it doesn't work." When Doug is home, Clint only wants dad to do what needs to be done for him. Mom can't; it doesn't matter that I tie his shoes, iron his clothes, give him his medication and vitamin pills, shave his sweet face, fill his tummy with good food...if dad is home, mom is just chopped liver. We both groaned. I told Clint that he had plenty of light, but what does mom know? So, once again Doug got up, found another bulb, fixed the nightlight, and finally Clint had LIGHT. Everything was right so Clint could sleep in peace.

Two thousand years ago God put a light in the sky to make everything right so mankind could have Peace (John 14:26). Do you know what would be great for all of us? It would be good for us if we could be like Clint: if our Light not working, so bothered that we could not sleep. If only, we would be so persistent that we would go to our Father and stand in His Presence until He did something. He will, because He is a faithful Father. He wants us to have Light and be Light. He knows the security, peace, and joy that is ours when we have light! It happens when we "receive" His Light: spiritual receptivity.

Do you want more light today? Be aware of His presence. Even as I was aware of my girls' presence, as I strung those Christmas lights, my heart filled with the joy of being with them. My "wattage" is determined by dozens of daily choices to choose Him. Seek Him. Praise Him. Rejoice in Him. Be aware of Him. Enjoying His Light is not some E.T. experience, it comes in the form of anticipating His presence. "Good Morning Father, this is the day You have made..." It is hearing His Word and living in response to it. It is stringing His thoughts like a strand of lights encircling my mind; wrapping my burdens and cares in the Light of His promises; and in all the dailiness of this life, reminding my heart that soon, we will be Home. Our Father will welcome us, and we will step into His presence of light and life, knowing all of it was prepared just for us!

42 HIDING GIFTS

Every time I get online there is a calendar showing me
how many days till Christmas! It's all around us,
clamoring for attention, demanding more gets done.
Well, here's a "Christmas thought" to take with you in
the midst of December's demands. I have been putting
the grandchildren and children's presents in the spare
bedroom. The pile is getting quite large, and I need a
visual to keep track of what I have for each person.
Never knowing when the little "munchkins" will be
dropping in, I have placed my biggest blanket over the
whole pile of bounty. I've covered all the gifts so if
someone should open the door "accidentally" they won't
see what we have in store for them. It's going to be a
great surprise! Every time I go in that room, I smile,
Every time I put one more perfect gift under the blanket,
I smile. I leave the room thinking about all the delight
they will get on Christmas; but they can't see it yet. I
bought some shake and zoom cars, what a racket they
make! I accidently placed something on one and jumped
out of my skin as it squawked and "burned rubber."
Then I laughed thinking of Jack, Wil, and Caleb's faces

when they open those. How fun to store up gifts for the ones we love!

Well, this is just what our Father is doing. He has a pile of treasure for His children. We can't see them yet. As a matter of fact, He tells me my eyes have not seen, what He hath prepared for me (Isaiah 64:4). For since the beginning of the world men have not heard nor perceived by the ear, neither hath the eye seen, Oh God, beside Thee, what He hath prepared for him that waiteth for Him. It is like waiting for Christmas! Paul echoes the refrain in 1 Corinthians 2:9, "Eye hath not seen, nor ear heard, neither have entered into the heart of man the things which God hath prepared for them that love Him." Wow! God's blanket covering those surprises must be very big! He must be smiling as He places more treasures in store for us. He too, must be anticipating that special moment when we will all be together to open them and squeal with delight!

I don't know where you hide your presents, but every time you add to the pile, as you get ready to wrap the treasures, let it remind you of the Best Gift of all, the Gift that "covered" all our sins. God's covering is VERY BIG! Then think about what He has in store just for you! Right now, it is a "no peeking" time but soon, very soon, it will be revealed! Love the giver of Gifts today.

43 CHRISTMAS

Christmas and surprise! They just go together; they're practically synonymous. Think of Mary; imagine her surprise as the angel appeared and told her she would give birth to the very Son of God!

Think of the shepherds' surprise. They were half asleep on the dark hillside, when the sky lit up with a host of heavenly beings, proclaiming, "Glory to God in the highest." Their next word always makes me smile, "Peace." They had just scared the wits out of those shepherds and then they said, "Peace to you."

At Christmas every child, is waiting to be surprised. They have been living in anticipation of tearing off the Christmas paper and being wondrously surprised by what they find.

My biggest surprise came on my 34th birthday, November 27, 1984. God blessed Doug and I with a new born son. The surprise was that he was born with Down syndrome. We were shocked with the surprise. I picked up the pieces of my broken heart; reminded myself of the truth that never changes, "God doeth all things well." Especially the things I don't understand. This was an opportunity to trust in the Lord with all my heart, and lean not unto my own understanding. In all my ways to acknowledge him, and he would direct my path (Proverbs 3:5-6).

From the time Clint was three weeks old until he was five years old we did daily physical therapy. He had exercises that strengthened his muscles. Had we not exercised his muscles would have become even weaker.

We turned his head back and forth, squeaked toys to make him turn and look, and taught him to raise his hands. We were always motivating him to reach and stretch; we taught him to hold, grasp and pull.

Every motor skill was learned through repetitive, daily exercise. And that was just the outward, physical exercise. In the beginning, we did not know what was going on mentally and emotionally behind those big, brown eyes.

He never had a bedtime in the early years. We kept him up and around as much noise and stimulation as possible; because the twins were just two years old, we had a lot of stimulus. I never waited for him to wake up in the morning, as soon as the girls were awake, I would awaken Clint.

You see I was "mom," but I didn't know if Clint knew I was his mom. And the most important thing was that

Clint would know me and know that I loved him with all my heart.

So every morning I would switch on the light and wait to see if he would respond. Then I would call his name, "Oh, Clint, good morning." I would watch and wait for a response. Then I would go beside his crib and reach over and turn him toward me, but I wouldn't pick him up. I'd stand there, arms outstretched waiting for him to reach up to me, wanting him to recognize me.

Each morning we followed the same routine day after day, week after week, with no real response evident; I only saw the learned reactions. But then one morning I turned on the lights, I called out his name, I stood beside his crib and watched as he turns his head. He shifted to his back and looked at me; spontaneously he smiled and lifted his hands toward me. He knew me! He knew I was his mom! He knew he was loved. I will never forget that moment.

Well, every day our Father in heaven turns the light on. This is the day the Lord has made. He waits for our response. Every day He comes along side and calls to us, "Come unto me all ye that are weary and heavy laden, I will give you rest." He waits for our response.

God doesn't want a manipulated, mechanical response. He doesn't want churchy exercises or a robotic Christian life. He wants genuine acknowledgment of who He is. He wants us to know how much He loves us. God is God, but He longs for His children to know Him as, "My God, my Father."

BROKEN THINGS

I love watching Doug fix broken things. He has certainty about the way he handles "stuff." When using hammers and drills, he doesn't fumble or miss like I do. I like watching and being with him as he repairs and mends. I like being his helper; I can't fix it, but I can hand him the finishing nails, the Phillips screw driver, and the Duct tape. Our friendship grows as he fixes things with his carpentry hands and I help.

Sometimes I feel like Clint must feel. I am not very fast, and sometimes when asked to get something I come back with the wrong item, or I cannot find what I am supposed to find. But I do my best and we stand back and look at what he fixed −and I helped-, and our relationship is sweeter and deeper because of it. It is my delight to tell him, "Doug you are just so good!"

Well, as I give my Heavenly Father the broken things of Kathy and Kathy's life, I am placing those broken things in His carpentry hands. As I stay there, I find in His presence a comradeship. His ways are perfect (Psalm 18:30)! Sometimes I cannot find or see what I am supposed to, yet even then He helps. Hebrews 13:21 tells us, "Make you perfect in every work to do His will…"

As I trust in Him, my Father does what only He can do. We stand together and look at His work. I am so thankful for His repair, His mending of me. God is so Good! Many times, I find the thing that was broken wasn't all that important, but it was my time with Him that deepened our friendship and strengthened my faith.

Dear reader, mankind is broken by sin. But God in His mercy makes a way to be whole. I pray that you personally know God's forgiveness and gift of salvation. Romans 10:9-10, 13: "That if though shalt confess with thy mouth the Lord Jesus, and shalt believe in thine heart that God hath raised Him from the dead, thou shalt be saved. For with the heart man believeth unto righteousness and with the mouth confession is made unto salvation...For whosoever shall call upon the name of the Lord shall be saved."

Yes, He does the repair work, the saving, because He is a loving Heavenly Father. After salvation, falling in love with Him goes past coming to Him just for help, just for fixing! As I spend time with Him, walking with Him, acknowledging Him in all my ways and moments, my soul finds its delight and whispers, "God, you are so good!"

ABOUT THE AUTHOR

Kathy Jackson is the wife of Dr. Douglas R. Jackson, and is the mother to twin daughters, Kristina and Katrina, and son, Clint.

Kathy serves the Lord alongside her husband, who this year, 2018, celebrates 40 years of pastoring at Community Baptist Church. Kathy is known for her sound Bible teaching and her helpful Christ-honoring insights as a ladies' speaker at retreats, camps, and conferences. Kathy has also used her artistic ability in black-light chalk art presentations to challenge ladies with biblical truth. Additionally, she teaches girls' chapel and art at Community Baptist Christian School.

Kristina serves with her husband, Aaron Wilson, at Camp CoBeAc, Prudenville, Mi. They have two energetic sons, Jackson and Wil.

Katrina serves with her husband, Daniel Bonner, at Community Baptist Church and School. They have three precious children, Katelyn, Autumn, and Caleb Douglas.

Clint, who was born with Down Syndrome in 1984, is actively involved with his parents at Community. Weekly he participates by ushering and visitation.

Made in the USA
Monee, IL
12 February 2022

90339419R00083